THE
COMPLETE GUIDE TO
PAINTBALL

SECOND EDITION

THE COMPLETE PAINT

PAINT

Written by Steve Davidson, Pete "Robbo" Robinson, Rob "Tyger" Rubin, and Stewart Smith

Special Contributions by Jerry Braun, Durty Dan, and Sarah Stevenson

Photographed by Peter Field Peck

Illustrations by Mark Smith

GUIDE ^{TO} BALL

The Complete Guide to Paintball
Second Edition

Written by Jerry Braun, Steve Davidson, Justin Owen, Pete "Robbo" Robinson, Rob "Tyger" Rubin, and Stewart Smith
Special Contributions by Durty Dan, and Sarah Stevenson
Photographed by Peter Field Peck
Illustrations by Mark Smith
Conceived by Andrew Flach
Researched by Tracy Tumminello

Adaptations of "Getting Started," "Rules to Play By," and "Common Mistakes," courtesy of splatterzone.com

The Complete Guide to Paintball
A GETFITNOW.com Book

Hatherleigh Press/GETFITNOW.com Books
An affiliate of W.W. Norton & Company, Inc.
5-22 46th Avenue, Suite 200
Long Island City, NY 11101

Visit our website: www.getfitnow.com

All Hatherleigh Press titles are available for bulk purchase, special promotions, and premiums. For more information, please contact the manager of our Special Sales Department at 1-800-528-2550.

Library of Congress Cataloging-in-Publication Data

The complete guide to paintball / written by Steve Davidson ... [et al.] ; special contributions by Jerry Braun, Durty Dan, and Sarah Stevenson ; photographed by Peter Field Peck ; illustrations by Mark Smith.—Rev. ed.
p. cm.
ISBN 1-57826-099-X
1. Paintball (Game) I. Davidson, Steve.

GV 1202.S87 C64 2002
796.2—dc21
2002027336

Photographed with Canon® cameras and lenses on Fuji® and Kodak® print and slide film
Text design and composition by edn Design
The text is set in Agenda

Printed on acid-free paper
10 9 8 7 6 5 4 3 2 1
Printed in Canada

"A friend of ours found this gun in an agricultural catalogue that was used by cattlemen to mark cows. It wasn't long afterwards that we bought two of these things and had ourselves a little duel. After it was over, we just knew we had stumbled upon something great."

- *Hayes Noel*

Acknowledgments

The editors and publisher are grateful to the following individuals for their assistance and encouragement in the publication of this book.

Jerry Braun and Paintball Sports International, for their endless help and support.

Cousins Paintball, for the use of their field in Medford, NY for our photo shoots. Paul Sattler, Fred Dorski, and Elio Napolitano, for giving so generously of their time and knowledge.

Jay Tavitian, and everyone at Oceanside Paintball, for showing us the time of our lives.

Sarah Stevenson, Karen Barber, and the entire 2 Die 4 team for their knowledge, enthusiasm and determination.

Cleo and Paul Fogal, for sharing their home, their field, and their story with us.

Mike Henry, Jim Lively, and Colin Thompson, for always leading us in the right direction.

NY Dogs, a great bunch of guys and a terrific team of paintball players. It was an honor playing with them.

Glenn Palmer, for always lending his assistance and equipment so willingly to this project.

Graham Easton, for helping outfit us for this paintball adventure.

Dawn and Bill Mills, of warpig.com for all their guidance and assistance.

Guy Cooper of Pro Star Sports, for his informative "Paintball Field Operator's Guide."

Steve Dunn and Extreme Adventures Canada, for the use of their Flak Jacket. It helped make Peter's job a little less painful.

National Paintball Supply, for the use of Squeegee Man.

The entire Wild Geese team, and especially Ralph Torrell, for sharing with us his extensive paintball gun collection.

Jim Della Constanza, for making Skyball such an enjoyable tournament.

Matthew Howard, for all his assistance with our Australian paintball directory.

We would also like to thank the following companies for generously loaning us equipment.

ADCO, Brass Eagle, Diablo, Diggers, JT, Kingman International, Lapco, Palmer's Pursuit Shop, Pro-Team Products, R. P. Scherer, Sheridan, Smart Parts, Soft Boards & Barriers Co., Tippmann Pneumatics, WDP, and Zap.

To everyone in the paintball industry — the players, manufacturers, field owners, distributors, and fans. We couldn't have written this book without your help and support. Thank you!

Contents

Part 3 GEAR

Part 4 DRILLS

Part 5 TACTICS

Second Edition Updates WHAT'S NEW AND WHAT'S HOT

APPENDIX

WHO IS THIS BOOK FOR?

This book is for everyone who plays or is interested in playing paintball. Everyone will appreciate the scope of this first edition; it is as much a tribute to the diversity within the game and its players as it is a guide. Regardless of your skill level, this book holds something for you.

We cover the fascinating history of the game (with firsthand accounts from its originators!), and the basic rules of the game (and descriptions of exciting variations on the paintball theme!). We offer in-depth equipment and gun information, and include essential tactical insights, as well as a thorough glossary and resource guide. Beginners and novices take note: Insights from the best players in the world make this book an ideal starting point for those of you serious about adding new dimensions of fun and excitement to your hobby and becoming great at this game.

For those of you who have played for a few years or are seasoned veterans, check out this book's authoritative analysis of guns and air systems, articles on advanced strategy, exclusive input on injury prevention stretches from former Navy SEAL, Stewart Smith, discussion of accessories, and comprehensive listing of international resources for both playing and purchasing equipment.

Our authoritative sections on the physics of paintball and guidelines for cleaning your gun correctly are among many gems in this book. We're sure that you'll find our interviews with great players both enlightening and useful in your search for competitive advantages. Motivated to elevate your game to the next level and beyond? Read on!

And then, of course, there are the pictures—visually arresting, dynamic shots taken by Peter Peck, who was himself "shot" innumerable times garnering these photographs. If you just love the game and want a book that captures the action, look no further.

Although we have attempted to be comprehensive, we realize that this volume is not the last word on the sport. For example, such luminaries as Jerry Braun, Bob Long, Jim Lively, and Dawn and Bill Mills of warpig.com gave of their time and shared insights that made this book possible. We would have loved to include more from them. We did not cover scenario games, a paintball format that we learned early on truly merits its own book. That said, we believe that we're off to a strong start. In the interest of ensuring that future editions raise the bar, we encourage you to contact us with your feedback about aspects of the game we ought to cover for the first time or in greater depth.

WHO IS PAINTBALL FOR?

For those of us who play paintball and love it, the question is what are you looking for in a game?

The answers that lead directly to paintball are listed below

If these are your answers, welcome home! This game is for you. Otherwise, you should read on. You just may want to change your mind.

I want fast-paced, totally immersive action.

There isn't a single, true standstill in paintball play, nor is there a moment where you don't feel like something is at stake. You are on offense and defense constantly, and your objectives require you to be alert and decisive—not hyper, mind you, just in the flow of the game. Opponents lurk around every corner and paintballs travel at up to 300 feet per second. You need to survive, but be willing to make a coordinated sacrifice to win the game for your team. Your teammates count on you to act with caution and precisely controlled aggression from one moment to the next. You can hear your competition moving toward you. You see paintballs flying and hear them splat against trees or barriers. You slide forward on your knees, dive behind a tree, cover your teammates' advance, celebrate victory after a hard-fought contest. Guaranteed to render "first-person, shoot'em-up, networkable computer simulations" a permanent second choice, paintball is the premiere action game.

I want a vigorous mental challenge as well as a rigorous physical one.

This is a thinking person's game. A lapse in concentration leads to elimination. If you're indoors, you may choose tactics based on speedy deployment with constant movement and firing in support of advances. If you're outdoors on a wide open field, you may want to split your force in two and converge on the enemy from opposite directions. To win at this game consistently, you and your team must use appropriate tactics while communicating (that means speaking and listening) coherently, and thinking quickly to adapt to the unexpected. It takes maturity to act as an individual without losing sight of your role in a team effort. It takes intelligence and quick decision making to prevail in the hair-raising scenarios that paintball presents.

I want a game I can play.

Except for the newborn, paintball is for everyone! The rules are straightforward, there are games and formats for every skill level, and the costs of playing are affordable. You can play the game with family and friends, with your church group, with corporate colleagues, or even go on your own simply to meet people who share your passion for intense, team-oriented sports. Whether things go well or not during your game, you will form a unique bond with whomever you play. And you can't make friends of strangers any faster than by playing paintball with them. It's safe to say that paintball is an unparalleled social experience, and open to all comers.

I want to be the best at whatever game I play.

If you put in the time and energy, form a great team, train together regularly, and have a little luck, you can become a professional paintball player, experience a tempo of game play that is unsurpassed, and vie for national and international championships against the best players in the world. For some, being a weekend warrior is enough. Others play for the thrill of victory, and seek out ever higher levels of competition. Paintball serves up plenty of opportunities for everyone. How far you go in this sport is largely up to you.

Whether you played tag or hide-and-seek when you were younger or yesterday, this game, in any of its manifestations, represents the most thrilling experience of competition you are likely ever to experience. Add to that the extraordinary comraderie you invariably develop with teammates, and you have one of the best games ever invented!

PAINTBALL IS FOR YOU!

Everybody wants to experience adventure—a highly intensified, dramatic realization of acting heroically and skillfully to attain a goal. We seek a sense of mission, of honoring our values, of taking advantage of opportunities that present themselves in our professional and romantic lives. Paintball is a microcosm of the adventure we experience each day. It crystallizes the sense of drama we seek to lend meaning to our choices and actions. Paintball taps into your imagination—*what if my life hinges on what I choose to do in the next moment?* Paintball provides a rapid succession of such moments that lead to an unparalleled gaming experience that is both universal and highly personal for every player. For those of you looking for a game that is more than the sum of its parts, here it is. Seize it!

WHO ARE WE?

The authors and interviewees are among the finest and most influential men and women ever involved with the game of paintball. For them, paintball is a passion of one sort or another. They share in common a singular devotion to the widespread enjoyment of this game, and that is why we sought their involvement with this endeavor. We think you'll be thrilled with the results.

The publisher of this book is a multifaceted multimedia company that perceived a unique opportunity to present an authoritative text on the subject of paintball to the game's growing base of enthusiastic participants, among whom we count ourselves.

GETFITNOW.com is an imprint of The Hatherleigh Company, Ltd. committed to developing multimedia health and fitness products for consumers of all ages. We believe that leading a healthy life-style can and should be a source of enjoyment and fulfillment. Paintball combines vigorous physical activity and tactical thinking in a way that we find irresistably fun.

You should go play this game as soon as possible.

—AWC

PART 1

WELCOME
to the Game of
PAINTBALL

Genesis of the Game

WHAT IS PAINTBALL REALLY ABOUT?

Paintball is an extraordinarily simple game in its basic form. A couple of people alternately hunt and evade one another, until one person or a team emerges triumphant over another. The victor is the first to achieve an objective or the last left standing. Yes, the game uses sophisticated technology, which is constantly evolving as people come up with new paintball accessories and gun mechanisms, and the specific objectives vary according to game designers' imaginations. But the basic game remains the same.

No matter what version of the game you find yourself most attracted to, its essence is constant. What is paintball's essence? The answer is two-fold.

Paintball is a Game

Paintball is, in the final analysis, one of many games people play with balls. In what is basically an advanced version of tag, the balls—gel-encased, water soluble goo—are propelled at up to 300 feet per second by a special, gas-powered gun. You *eliminate* (tag) opponents when paintballs you or your teammates shoot hit and break on them. Simple, right? And, as with any game, the whole point of it is to have a good time in a competitive context. Like football, basketball, and baseball, elements of paintball require players to acquire and practice certain skills. Like these other games, it has rules, some hard and fast and others that are subject to interpretation. It shares in common with more free form activities, like skateboarding and surfing, built-in enthusiasm for innovation, personal style, fast-thinking, and highly individualistic approaches. As the people who played the first game did, anyone can come up with their own version of the game. Once

**Smart-thinking,
alert and precise action,
and good fortune
lead to victory**

with other people—family, friends, coworkers who are our team members. There is no escaping the fact that however well we may do on our own, we lead more fulfilling lives when we spend time in meaningful pursuits with others who share our values and goals.

Especially in America, with our culture of "manifest destiny," and the "American Dream," we are hard-wired with an optimistic and moral sense that people should put forth their best effort, go for it, "just do it," when it comes to just about everything in life. We attach importance not only to our goals, but how we achieve them.

**Be honest. Don't lie.
Be considerate. Don't be violent.
Follow the rules. Don't cheat.
Be creative. Don't be predictable.
Have fun. Don't have a negative outlook.
Be a team player. Don't be egotistical.
Be resilient. Don't ever give up.**

you're equipped with the essential safety equipment, there is enormous room for having your own kind of fun with this game.

Paintball is About Survival

Paintball is also more than just a game. At its most exhilarating moments, it is an intensified version of what people do everyday. With varying degrees of success, we're all avoiding and confronting obstacles on our way to reaching goals. This is the case whether you're in school or pursuing a career, a man or a woman, regardless of your beliefs or ethnicity.

We're all survivors. We all have goals that we're in different stages of reaching. We take risks. We learn from our mistakes and get back into the fray. We improve at the skills necessary to meet daily objectives and lifelong dreams. We do all of this

Of course, these are things all people value, not just Americans. They work for everybody in all situations. But it is no accident that paintball was created in America.

Paintball captures the essence of the basic struggle of every living being. Staying in the game is the most obvious metaphor for staying alive. And winning is about being great at surviving while vanquishing foes in fair play.

The game of paintball creates a situation in which the only way to survive is to act in manner that balances precise aggression with caution. You attain objectives by taking risks that you have a good chance of handling.

Being great at paintball requires you to learn how to take great risks and succeed.

Welcome to the Game of Paintball

It is also a very physical game, and to play it well means executing moves quickly and dynamically. The height of game play is achieved by mastering basic techniques and tactics, improvising effectively, working well with a team, and being fit.

The notion of paintball as a test of survival skills is what inspired its progenitors, Hayes Noel and Charles Gaines.

BIG QUESTIONS

A little less than 20 years ago, these two very close friends discovered a way to test ideas they had debated extensively during their relationship. *Are we born with all the resources we need to survive, or do we learn how to survive in response to our environment? Are survival skills learned in one context portable to other contexts? How does a person's tolerance for risk affect his ability to prevail in adverse conditions? What is the relationship between honesty and survival?* To address these tremendous questions, Noel and Gaines devised a game they called, simply, "survival." Today, we know that game as paintball. When you play, give a moment's thought to the questions this game was first invented and played to resolve. What are your answers? You can learn more about what the founders were thinking in their interviews in this book.

FROM "THE NATIONAL SURVIVAL GAME" TO TODAY

Seizing a unique opportunity to turn the game into a profitable business model, Noel and Gaines teamed up with a friend, Bob Gurnsey, and started selling marking guns and paint, and access to fields where people could get together to play the survival game. The first guns—"Splatmasters"—were made by the Nelson Paint Company, which actually had the guns manufactured under contract by the Daisy Manufacturing Company Incorporated. They made up rules for simple games like Capture the Flag and Total Elimination. This was the birth of the first paintball franchise, The National Survival Game, and what would grow to a 800 million dollar industry.

Soon other franchises emerged that started to experiment with new kinds of team games. New technologies and the development of unique paintball products dramatically accelerated the evolution of multiple paintball formats, from recreational play to scenario games, from amateur tournaments to professional, international championships.

The game has undergone dramatic changes over the years. If you look closely, however, you'll see that its essence has survived.

—AWC

Walking through the woods one day...

The actual genesis of the game really started in my mind on a walk through the woods of Virginia with a friend of mine who lives in Charlottesville and has a farm there. We were walking through the farm and he was talking about hunting wild buffalo. I'm not a hunter myself, but I was enthralled by his story. He was talking about hunting buffalo in Africa and how he was in these bulrushes and couldn't see the beasts but could hear them, about having to be aware of wind direction, about the feelings he had experienced in this extreme scenario.

I was really caught up in the thrill and the excitement and the high that he clearly had felt doing that kind of thing. The severity of the situation he was describing, the notion of survival being boiled down to a few decisive moments, just blew me away. This was 1976 and I was 35 years old. I said, "Why don't we just stalk and hunt each other on the way back to the house?" I'd done this as a kid, playing cowboys and Indians and things. But somehow the context of his story made me feel like more was at stake, and I had this remarkable adrenaline rush. I didn't forget it when I returned to New York City where I lived for 15 years making my living trading the markets on the American Stock Exchange.

I used to go to New Hampshire about once every two months to see Charles Gaines, who's one of my best friends, as well as a big outdoorsman, hunter, writer... a guy just totally at home in the wilderness.

Charles said something like, "You know, if I ever got you in the woods you'd be dead meat in a second." So we began a conversation and then sort of a debate over almost a year and half about surviving in the wilderness and what qualities it would take.

I told him that if I could survive in the Wall Street jungle, I would survive in any jungle. Charles thought this was nonsense, but I was convinced that survival skills were transportable across environments. For example, to my way of thinking tolerance for risk-taking, aggressive and defensive tendencies, a tempo of decision making and action are things that one masters in order to excel in any context. Charles believed that survival skills were inextricably linked to context, and could be learned or acquired in one environment without the benefits accruing to experiences in others. So I could be great on Wall Street, but would be devoured in the forest. Needless to say, this was a great debate.

We'd read Richard Connell's "The Most Dangerous Game" in high school and stuff like that always really turned us on. And then we were in the midst of this debate for over a year and half, and gradually over the course of our conversations we tried to devise good survival tests. And maybe with that story kicking around subconsciously somewhere in there, we developed a sense that we needed a hunting game to test our theories.

But we really never could come up with anything, until a friend of ours, George Butler, found this paintball gun in an agricultural catalogue that was used by cattlemen to mark cows. It wasn't long afterwards that we bought two of these things and had ourselves a little duel. After it was over, we just knew that we had stumbled upon something great. Almost right away we were talking about the potential for games based on survival using this kind of gun.

—Excerpt from interview with Adam W. Cohen

Hayes Noel currently trades the markets in Santa Cruz, CA, where he lives with his wife and two children.

PAINTBALL AT GROUND ZERO

Hayes Noel

ADAM COHEN: So who won that first duel?

HAYES NOEL: [Laughs] Charles did. He's a much better shot than I am. In fact, he shot me directly in the ass. [Laughs] I was wearing a bathing suit. We didn't have goggles or any protective gear, but what did we know. We were just thrilled to be doing this finally. I shot at him first and missed. Then he got me in the butt. His shot raised a little welt, which stung for a while. As far as I was concerned, that just made it more realistic.

We could see right then that we had the tool we needed to play this kind of hunting game that we wanted, because it wasn't like these tomato wars that they have in New Hampshire or Vermont. These guns were fairly accurate and could really tag you from quite a distance away. So they were sort of like guns without the danger of guns.

Not long after the duel, we played a little stalking game out in one of the wooded fields around his house. I was ecstatic because I knew that now we could play these awesome games whenever we wanted.

So then Bob Gurnsey got involved in it when we started to formulate the rules and an idea of the game. The three of us spent another six months arguing about the rules, and how a large-scale competitive version of the game would be structured.

We had decided to invite 9 different people that we knew to join us and play this game. The participants were from all over the country, people who were successful in whatever they had undertaken to accomplish. For example, we invited a guy from Alabama, who was one of the best wild turkey guides and hunters in the sport. We had two guys who had been long-range reconnaissance patrol leaders in Vietnam. Among the others were a lawyer or two, a doctor from Chicago, a movie producer from Los Angeles, and the outdoor writer for Sports Illustrated who had been cleared to do an article on the game.

The mix of people was exciting. Some were local New Hampshire friends of Charles. The man who eventually won, Richard White, was a local lumber man and deer hunter.

Anyway, we took this 80 acre cross-country ski area, filled with second growth woods. You could see through it. There were trails and it was clear enough that you could move pretty well through these woods. We marked off the boundaries of the space and appointed a responsible friend of ours to be head judge.

So we had these four flag stations. In each flag station there were 12 flags of the same color, one for each player. So there was one flag station with 12 blue flags just hanging out in the open and others with 12 green flags, 12 yellow flags, and 12 red flags. Each flag station had a judge with a whistle.

At 10 o'clock in the morning, we positioned people at equal distances apart along the circumference of the area. Some guy fired a shotgun and it started.

The first person to go in and get one flag of each color and get back out without being shot won the game as soon as he reached the home base where the head judge was waiting. We didn't know how long it would take. Everybody had a different color paint, so you could tell who shot you by color. And if you got any paint on you at all, even splatter from a hit on a tree, you were out. That's not the way it's done now, but that was the way that we did it then. Everybody was cammoed up and looked really intense. I'm certain that observers would be simultaneously a little bothered and titillated by the militant look. We weren't striving for that. We were just wearing what made sense to wear when you're running around in the woods trying not to be seen.

they do. They'd sell a lot of paintballs at the field level.

However, in order to get sponsorship and TV revenue and live gate revenue, in order to put asses in the seats, so to speak, you have to make it viewer friendly. Right now, it's not a viewer friendly sport. And so you look at the magazines that come out and this and that, and all the advertisers are basically people who are producing products that people who play the game use and I think the only people that buy the magazines are people who play the game.

Whoever gets paintball on TV will make as much money as all the people selling all the paint and guns that exist today.

But, you know, that's not where they're at right now. They want to sit around and debate about whether to shoot 23 balls or ten balls. And to a certain extent they're not wrong to do so. 14-year-old boys want the best paintball gun money can buy for Christmas, and that's the market they're serving.

ADAM: Any final thoughts on the game, your sense of its essence, what you love about it?

HAYES: Have you seen "Life is Beautiful?"

ADAM: Yes, I have.

HAYES: That character was a survivor. I thought it was a great movie, that it dealt with the holocaust from the standpoint of a survivor. I felt the movie was about the perseverance of an individual in the face of this total horror. His humor, his resilience, his creativity, his courage-he was a total survivor. And I'm not saying that people who didn't survive somehow didn't measure up. Obviously, not. It's just that here was this guy doing everything he could to save his family. And at any moment, his luck could have run out, but he made sure that as far as he had anything to do with it, could have any control over what might happen, his son would live. And even though he

dies, he wins. That guy would have won our first game.

ADAM: Interesting.

HAYES: I don't even know why I'm bringing this up, except to say, that really, to me, this survival game is about whoever does well in the individual game. I'm not trying to be too heavy about it, but you know, a guy from the hills of Tennessee or a guy on Madison Avenue in New York is just as likely to have the qualities of a survivor as not.

This was an extraordinary man who, however he did it, faced this horror, dealt with it, and saved his genes. I don't know, I just thought it was very moving, a great movie.

So I wouldn't say a country or city boy is a better survivor than the other.

ADAM: It's the individual.

HAYES: Absolutely.

ADAM: Got it. Do you ever actually get together with these guys and just play the survival game, because just listening to you talk, it's hard to picture you enjoying the team approach much.

HAYES: No, I never did it in a recreational way. And honestly, to be on the floor of the American Stock exchange...

The thing is I used to love to play poker, and once I started trading the market by myself, I never played poker anymore. I know better than anybody who I know of what risk is. I get to take 50 risks a day if I want to. Or 20 risks or 10 or five. I get to practice what it feels like all the time. This is an important thing about survival games.

This wasn't initially why I wanted to start paintball, but it was very clear to me that because of the illusion of danger that you create in the game, it allows people to feel what it feels like to take risks.

ADAM: People don't usually like that feeling,

but they're enticed by it.

HAYES: No, they don't like it at all. It's the same feeling whether you're falling in love or whether you're making a commitment, a real commitment to something or whether you're taking a financial risk. People don't really like that feeling.

At some point, you have to learn that on the other side of risk is growth and not death. It's one of T.S. Elliot's points in "The Wasteland." Between the thought and the action falls the shadow—between the conception and realization falls the shadow. The shadow is the personal fear that people feel, the anxiety they feel, and it's a physical feeling, in all of these things. I think it's an actual physical anxiety that people feel. You need to practice getting through that.

So I don't really play paintball anymore. Except for that first game, the survival game, which was so new. But I do "play" every day.

ADAM: Understood. Thank you for your time, Hayes.

HAYES: You bet.

The Attraction of Paintball

Jerry Braun

A Game for Children of All Ages

Stop and think about the very first games you ever played. There are two games most of us played as children. One of them was Follow the Leader. The other one was a primal hunt and chase game, such as tag or hide-and-seek. You can be Chinese, you can be Venezuelan, you can be American, you can be Aleutian, you can be anyone from anywhere in the world. These are games you have played, the ones you started with, the ones you associate with being a child bursting with energy.

Remember when you were a kid playing hide-and-seek? Your heart would be in your mouth because your friend was three feet away from you and was just about to find you out. You felt that the world was going to come to an end if you were discovered. Remember playing tag? There was always a safe spot, but you'd leave it and run as hard as you could in order not to get tagged. Sometimes you'd run behind an obstacle to gain time. The exhilaration of not being found or tagging another player is what you experience playing paintball. That is why it is so appealing.

Now, some of us pretend it isn't so, but human beings, like most animals, have predatory instincts. Look at the very first games played by kittens and puppies, they are primal hunt-and-chase games. They stalk each other, bat at and chew on each other. Basically, they playfully attack one another. Pure play is nature's way of teaching survival. Playing paintball triggers the same kinds of responses in humans, except that we don't have to learn how to "go for the jugular" to survive the way animals do. So our enjoyment of games like paintball is a little different than theirs.

Jerry Braun, 4th from left in back row, at Skyball 1999, Toronto, Canada.

People talk about the game being violent. No doubt the images of adults brandishing guns looks intimidating and suggests violence. The basic characteristics of violence—the use of force to destroy or hurt others and a chaotic lack of structure that promotes reckless and dangerous behavior—are simply nowhere to be found in paintball. The objectives never involve hurting people, and the rules are clear and enforced. Nothing like the bench-clearing brawls that occur in professional baseball or hockey ever occurs in amateur or professional paintball.

When you first play the game, it elicits emotions in you that you may not have experienced since you were 3 years old. It's a sophisticated game of tag, except that it doesn't involve physical contact, incorporates teamwork, and frequently involves objectives beyond eliminating your opponent . And the pure joy you see on the faces of kids playing tag, that's what paintball provides. That's why people who play it once usually come back for more.

Charles Gaines

ADAM COHEN: Do you think the skills that you acquire and develop by playing paintball are applicable to everyday real-life experiences?

CHARLES GAINES: Absolutely! More to the point, I think the survival game, as it was played back when Hayes [Noel] and I played it, is illuminating for anyone who plays it. Unlike Hayes who held that people are born with certain survival skills, I think that for the most part, we learn them based on our will to immerse ourselves in an environment and discover it. And so the game is a way of finding out about yourself...if you want it to be. I can't say too much about the game as it's played today, because I haven't played it recently and it's definitely changed. But I imagine from what I read about it and hear about it, that at the very least, the game's essential experience still heightens your awareness of yourself as a survivor in a specific context. Your ability to win is related to your receptiveness to the details and the nuances of your surroundings and your response to the scenario you're in. So I do believe that it's true that you can take lessons learned in the midst of playing any version of paintball, and apply those to improving your everyday life.

ADAM: Knowledge is power, and what you learn in paintball is often very personal knowledge. In terms of risk-taking, in terms of learning about how you function under pressure, in terms of making quick decisions, in terms of communicating with others effectively. You agree?

CHARLES: It's true. The survival game is like a little paradigm for real life. You know, it's more this way with the original game. After all, we play life as individuals, not as a team, regardless of our social experience. I mean, you can be part of a team in a business or family, but we're all individuals and we play life that way. Each of us has to make decisions

and live with the consequences of acting on them.

I believe that the initial game, the every-man-for-himself format, was more paradigmatic of life than the team game. But, of course, both of them are nice paradigms. The point is always to succeed at what you're trying to do. And either alone or as part of a team, you have to act.

ADAM: The responsibility is still on each individual in the team game. Especially at the pace that the team game is played today, "teamwork" is really driven by individual actions that are more implicitly than explicitly coordinated.

CHARLES: That's how the initial paradigm plays out in today's game. Of course, in life, you're trying to make something of yourself. You're trying to succeed at making money or becoming happy or famous or all of these things. And accomplishing these things means taking steps. In the survival game, you're trying to succeed at a very limited task. You know, in the case of the team game, you go in and grab the other team's flag. In the case of the individual game, the way we played it, you grab all four flags and get out without being put out of the game. These are great metaphors for staying alive that are impossible to ignore, especially for first time players.

If you're smart about it, you bring to both the game and your life who you really are. You don't try to fake it. In other words, the people who got put out the quickest and the easiest in the game when I played it were people who were trying to be something other than what they were, the one who pretended to have talents and skills that they didn't actually own. Being good at this game means being willing to play within yourself.

ADAM: Like a baseball pitcher in a clutch situation, you shouldn't throw a pitch you can't handle.

CHARLES: Exactly. But then you learn new

pitches and start working them in as you get better at them. I think that may be the deepest and most piercing truth that overlaps playing paintball and playing at real life. All we know after a certain age in life is that the only way to achieve success is to be who we are, to rely on our real strengths, not our perceived or dreamed about strengths. And to play honestly. That was one of the things that we learned very early on about the game.

Now, I don't know if any of these things relate as profoundly anymore to the current game. I just literally don't know. I haven't played it and I don't even know how it's played. I hope it's the case. But the original game, the reason it was so resonant and the reason it was so much fun for us, was that it was so clear from the very beginning that we were doing something that really was alive with these metaphorical implications we're talking about now. You really teach yourself something about who you are, where you are, and something about the condition of life.

ADAM: Awesome. I completely understand what you mean. It's basically the kind of experience you have when you're faced with an extreme challenge and you have to rely on yourself to succeed.

CHARLES: That's it.

ADAM: And you know in that moment that whether or not you succeed is going to require you to keep your cool, keep focused, and simultaneously go for it. I mean it's a higher level of alertness. For me it comes in situations where I've been in sports competitions, or acting on stage, or speaking in public. Anytime I'm pushing myself.

CHARLES: Right. And so much of it has to do with timing, which is another thing that you learn in life. You can make the same choice at two different times and one time you'll be successful and the other time it'll cost you big time.

ADAM: Right. Having spoken with a number of people who are in the game now, I can say, that it has lost this sort of philosophical edge. I wouldn't say the game itself isn't enjoyable as it's being presented now. It's just not what it was for you guys, an experiment, playing with ideas of survival. It's a business now, a diversion, recreation, entertainment. You have any comments on that.

CHARLES: Yeah. That's the way I perceive it to be. And it's one of the reasons for my sort of inattention to the game in its present version. But I bet that the idea of surviving is still a factor, still part of the attraction of the game.

I mean, as far as I'm concerned, we who founded it had it at its very best. After we invented it, we started playing on a regular basis, both the individual game and more and more the team game. We had a field that we rented out, or borrowed. My kids played it, and my wife played it once and [Bob] Gurnsey's kids played it and we had our children out there acting as field judges. We'd make whole weekends out of this thing. And it was just joyous and wonderful. Good, simple fun with friends and family.

We'd have people come up from New York and out from Los Angeles to play the game. They would play it for the first time and immediately "grok" it and see how cool it was. I had my friend P.J. O'Rourke up to play it and he loved it.

It was great because it started as our little secret game. And then we introduced it to the world, which was like telling a very witty joke or some marvelously resonant parable for the first time. People could really see what we were talking about, especially after they played it. They'd say, "Ah, yes. Exactly. I get it. This is so cool!"

But then, we and the game were attacked by people who never played it but assumed that the presence of paintball guns somehow supported violence. Of course, in football and hockey, where they show highlights of people knocking each other's heads off, this criticism is virtually nonexistent. We had to fight this bad reputation that we really didn't deserve. And the business became somewhat difficult for me. The commercialization of the game, which literally turned it into what I perceive to be little more than shooting each other in the woods, cost me my entire interest in it.

ADAM: It turned into a team game when you started to turn it into a business, basically.

CHARLES: Yeah. That's right. But initially, we wanted it to be both a team and an individual game. But the individual game just sort of died out, out of lack of interest.

ADAM: That's mystifying.

CHARLES: Yeah, I thought so. I mean, to me it's a much more interesting version of the game. And would continue to be, I think. Maybe nobody even knows about it anymore. I don't know. But to me it would still be a more interesting version even given the high powered guns and the maga-

zines that hold hundreds of paintballs. Given all of that it seems to me it would be more interesting than the team version.

ADAM: Well, you know, maybe it'll come back.

CHARLES: Maybe it will. That would be great.

Charles Gaines is an extraordinarily prolific and accomplished writer, published in magazines ranging from American Sportsman *and* Forbes F.Y.I. *to* Architectural Digest *and* Men's Journal. *He has also written various books, most recently,* Survival Games (1997). *He was also author of the international bestseller,* Pumping Iron (1974), *and Associate Producer of the film based on the book,* starring Arnold Schwarzenegger. He and his wife of 37 years currently live in Nova Scotia.

PAINTBALL EVOLUTION

ADAM COHEN: Steve, it's great to have a chance to sit down with someone who has been around the sport for as long as you have.

STEVE DAVIDSON: Thank you for having me.

ADAM: Let's jump right into the thick of things.

STEVE: Sure. Where would you like to begin?

ADAM: Everyone has their own take on the initial game. What do you make of it?

STEVE: Yeah, the story's kind of become the game's creation myth. A couple of guys had a debate about survival skills, and agreed on a way of settling it by playing a free-for-all version of capture the flag. The fact that a forester won without ever firing a shot is significant. It's a true story, and it's a simple one that tells you what the game is all about.

ADAM: The fact that being the last one standing isn't just about shooting loads of paint.

STEVE: Yes.

ADAM: Let's discuss how the game became widespread. That's what we're really interested in learning more about from you.

STEVE: Okay. Well, after that first game, these three guys, Hayes Noel, Charles Gaines, and Bob Gurnsey knew that this could become something more than a free-for-all recreational activity. They saw an entrepreneurial opportunity. They went to a couple of different companies and attempted to have a gun made specifically for playing the game. They eventually had "Splatmaster" manufactured and they went to the company that had made the original gun that they'd used, which was the "Nelspot Marker" made by Nelson Paint Company, to get the paint, which was oil-based. This was within months of that first game.

I did play a couple of games when the oil-based paint was still around, and boy are we all glad that was short-lived.

ADAM: Pretty disgusting, I take it?

STEVE: We're talking turpentine parties after every game, or just burning your clothes. But it was

STEVE DAVIDSON'S PAINTBALL BIOGRAPHY

When Steve Davidson began playing paintball in 1983, he fell in love with the game.

1983	Began playing paintball
1984	Formed Muthers of Destruction team
1986	IPPA representative for NJ & Coordinator of Team Registration program
	First article printed in APG magazine—*10 Ways to Becoming a Better Team Captain*
1989	Columnist for Paintball Sports International, PaintCheck & Paintball News; Forms Werewolves competition team
1990	Introduces team rankings & seedings; ranking & seeding services for World Cup, Lively Masters, ASO series, Paintcheck 5 Player & other events; Forms World Paintball Federation
1991	Authors, *MAXING: A Guide to Winning in Tournament Play*
1992	Organizes National Professional Paintball League
1996	Secretary, NPPL
1997	Forms GTO tournament series
1999	Introduces United States Paintball League patented game format (visit getfitnow.com for more details!)

fun. I wouldn't change the way it was then, but I'm glad we're using water-soluble food dyes now.

Anyway, they started franchising the game across the country. Jerry Braun in upstate New York was one of the first franchises, as was Deborah Dion out in Pittsburgh.

Around that same time it didn't take more than maybe about nine months there were at least two other franchise corporations on the scene. One was based in Florida called the "Ultimate Game" and the other was Pursuit Marketing Incorporated (PMI), which remains one of the biggest and best

distributors in the industry today.

National Survival Game (NSG) had a turnkey type of an operation: "We will supply you with the paint, with the guns, with the goggles, the rules of play, the insurance, and show you how to set a game up."

You had to buy everything from them. Until some far-thinking individuals said, "I ought to be able to find something similar elsewhere for less." People approached Nelson directly, and they had no hard core exclusivity agreement with NSG. Before you knew it, Skirmish USA, Paul Fogal's company, entered the scene. Fogal had approached NSG, but they couldn't work things out. He basically said, "No way," to their rates and went and started searching for other suppliers. He hooked up with Jeff Perlmutter from PMI.

Ultimate Game didn't last. They got crushed in what I call the Franchise Wars. NSG eventually went away because they remained, I guess the word would be "hidebound." They had a vision of what they thought the game should be and how it should be played and what you should use and how it should be organized. They weren't really interested in adjusting themselves to changes in the industry.

ADAM: Are we still in 1981?

STEVE: We're still in 1981, but we're kind of talking about stuff that happened between then and 1983. Specific dates on these things, I can't give you.

ADAM: NSG goes south within the first three years?

STEVE: They were still around and doing well, but they didn't have an adaptive long-term strategy. All of these independent fields were popping up all over the place. Then, Perlmutter introduced the water-soluble paintball. That opened things up for a large number of people. Abolishing the need for turpentine parties was progress.

NSG also had a tournament series and you could only qualify for this tournament series by finishing first or maybe second-place at a regional tournament that was held at an affiliated NSG field. So, for the first couple of years, the only tournaments were being played by NSG teams or maybe local stuff, but not on a national basis.

In 1986, Fogal had his first major national tournament with Perlmutter, and Jerry Braun had the Air Pistol Open. The word "Open" is what's significant there because any team, whether they were coming from an NSG field or not, could enter this event. That was a major step toward opening up the game across the board.

ADAM: And technologically?

STEVE: Tech-wise, the mid-eighties were explosive. During 1981, 1982, and the first half of 1983, people were playing with paintball guns that were hand-cocked, single-shot, twelve gram deals. Nelson's Nelspot 007, NSG's Splatmaster, and Benjamin Sheridan's PGP were the three that you had available to you. They were all tilt-feed/gravity-feed types of things.

At the end of 1983, people started putting pumps on the Nelspots and PGPs. The plastic Spotmarker from NSG became basically a low-cost, field rental piece of equipment and the "Tech Wars" started to pick up steam. Very shortly after the pump was first introduced, and this is still 1983/1984, Constant Air (CA) came out. Some ingenious people figured that there had to be a way to hook a larger canister of air up to their gun. They found a way to do it and, bang, they were immediately banned from tournament play. which slowed things down tremendously for a good couple of years.

ADAM: Were they welcome at Jerry's Opens, or not even those?

STEVE: No, absolutely not. People, including me, fought it viciously. To us, the whole game, the nature of the competition, was about to change radically. If we allowed those guns in tournament play, everything would be different. The simple necessity of having to change those twelve grams after twenty or thirty shots maximum, the necessity of having to carry that stuff, of not being able to stand there for fifteen minutes, made the game a certain, special kind of experience.

ADAM: So you weren't opposed to the CA technology *per se*. You just wanted the competition to be driven by tactics rather than guns.

STEVE: That was the issue. There were people out in California in particular who had gone the Constant Air route. Interest-

ingly enough, the Iron Men, who are one of the top teams now, were originally a CA team. They beat everybody, left right and center in California, but they didn't do any of the tournaments because they didn't want to give up their CA. They were the best team in the country at the time, but they couldn't prove it because they weren't willing to compete on the level that all the competition teams were.

Gravity Feeds came in right after the pump—again, the end of 1983, beginning of 1984—PVC pipe and a forty-five degree elbow. Then, around the middle of 1984 Gramps and Grizzly's started producing guns that came with those features standard.

ADAM: So the technology was driven by recreational play? It seems that way because the tournaments resisted these new tech features, but they were selling well to the rec players who were in the game for the fun of it.

STEVE: Sort of. It's interesting because you'd go to the tournament and you'd sit there and talk about all the nifty things that you could do to your gun, or that you were planning on doing to your gun, or that somebody else was thinking about doing to their gun.

We all recognized that there had to be some kind of a leveler at the tournaments. A bunch of people who were more into military simulation than they were

The guns on the next few pages are identified by manufacturer, type and description, in this order.

Carter; Buzzard; Top Level custom made tournament pump gun. Includes Smart Parts barrel. *Courtesy of Ralph Torrell*

Gotcha; Deuce; Double barrel stock gun with two-step trigger. *Courtesy of Ralph Torrell*

Palmer's Pursuit Shop; Nasty Typhoon; Customized double barrel semi with muzzle brake, double finger trigger, cosmetic trigger guard, bottleline with mounting brackets, and iodized blue. *Courtesy of Ralph Torrell*

Airgun Designs; Sydearm; *Courtesy of Ralph Torrell*

Nelson Paintball Company; Nelspot 007; 12 gram pump gun. *Courtesy of Rob Rubin*

Nelspot 007 with grip removed showing 12 gram CO_2 cartridge.

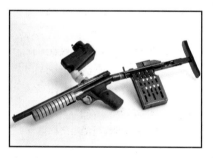

Sheridan; Piranha; Pump gun with 12 gram six pack from AirGun Designs, Inc. *Courtesy of Rob Rubin*

Detail of six pack.

paintball were trying to get things like smoke grenades and hand grenades and walkie-talkies and heavier weaponry introduced into tournament play. In response to this, Fogal was the one who put it the best: "We can count on the fact that every paintball player is going to have a gun, but if we start asking everybody to have to bring forty smoke grenades and radios and all this other kind of stuff, we're just going to price ourselves right out of the market. So we have to make a conscious effort to cut it off somewhere. Where should that cutoff be?"

Things went back and forth for a while. Jerry limited the barrels to ten inches; you couldn't have a barrel more than ten inches long.

ADAM: That doesn't make too much of a difference, does it?

STEVE: No, it doesn't make a difference. But we were trying everything. People were trying to sneak that kind of stuff in all the time.

There was a huge fuss over back check valves, these things that keep the pressure in the gun even when you remove the twelve gram or the bottle from it. It made it so you could remove your gas source and still have five or six or seven shots left in the gun. That was a big deal because we trained ourselves to listen for low air levels. You'd think to yourself: "He's about to change twelve grams, so we're going to rush him and take

him out." Well, if I'm that guy running low and I've got a back check valve, baby am I ever waiting for you to come at me. I'm going to make the biggest, most obvious twelve gram change that I possibly can. Some cocky guy's going to charge me, hopefully with all of his friends, and I'm going to take'm out. "Boink, boink, boink! See you all later. Thank you for listening!"

ADAM: Back checks sound very cool. Did they survive?

STEVE: No, those were banned. That little extra ability seemed to us like tinkering with the game, and we wanted to keep things very balanced and clear in terms of the mental and physical requirements.

ADAM: So the back check valve came along in 1984. 1984 seems like a big year for the game.

STEVE: It was a huge year for paintball technology. Absolutely. A lot of stuff was introduced in 1984. The back check valve came along with the CA.

Another big thing was a barrel extender. You take a piece of aluminum, stick it on the end of your barrel, and you have a longer barrel. Now, what that did for anybody? To this day, we still don't know. But somebody brought out the first barrel extender and they sold like hot cakes. So somebody else said, "Well, I'm going to come out with a field strip screw set for the gun," and people were begin-

There are many different kinds of goggles, and some are bound to fit you better than others, both physically and monetarily. We recommend trying on different kinds before making a purchasing decision.

Is that a gun in your pocket or...

Firepower

The second most important piece of equipment is your paintball gun, sometimes referred to as a marker because it literally marks other players. For the purposes of this book, guns are used only to shoot paintballs (and wouldn't it be a better world if that were the case). As you'll see, guns come in all shapes and sizes, but employ very similar firing mechanisms.

Main Body

The main body or frame of the gun is the handle, trigger, and the chamber, which contains the cocking mechanism and the bolt.

Some guns give you the option of attaching your own barrels and different sized hoppers and compressed air. The chamber or breech is where the ball awaits the rush of air that fires it when you pull the trigger. Near the chamber is something called a *ball detent*. This mechanism holds the paintball in place so it doesn't roll out. It also stops more than one ball from feeding into the chamber. The paintball is fired out of the chamber and through the barrel. The barrel is a long tube that guides the paintball in a straight path as it leaves the gun. There are many styles available and they screw into the main body. Many say that brass barrels are the best because they have the least friction on the paintball (they are the cheapest). Others swear by heavier stainless steel barrels. Some only play with aluminum. A lot of designs have holes (called porting)drilled into them in different patterns.

Keep the ammo coming!

Hopper or Loader

Basically a hopper is a plastic inverted bottle that holds your paintballs and allows them to feed into the chamber. Most hoppers rely on a gravity feed approach. Some however, are motorized and ensure that another paintball will fall into place after one is shot. If rapid firing is key to your game, make sure you have one of these.

Hoppers come in all sorts of sizes, some hold only 40 balls, while others can hold up to 300. The range of sizes is as follows (60, 80, 100, 130, 150, 200, 230, 300). Of course, by the time you read this, larger sizes may be available. Smaller hoppers are lighter, but carry fewer balls, creating that possibility of being caught short at the worst possible moment. The larger the hopper, the more balls you can fire before having to reload. Of course, this also makes the gun itself heavier. Most experienced players gravitate toward the large hoppers.

Bringing on the air!

Air Power

The air tank is crucial. On most guns, it attaches horizontally off the back of the gun, and literally screws on. Some players prefer a vertical mount to keep liquid CO_2, which is an inevitable and potentially very annoying byproduct of firing, on the bottom of the tank away from the gun. The most common propellant used in paintball is CO_2. Almost all fields supply a tank with their rental guns. Other propellants include nitrogen and high pressure air (HPA). HPA is just regular air. The great thing about it is that it won't freeze or turn to liquid in the cold like CO_2 and nitrogen. HPA containers have very high pressures (as high as 4500 psi).

Most of the tanks are currently made of aluminum, which is preferred to steel because it is lighter. More expensive air tanks enable you to check the status of your air reserves. Some of the more elaborate models can even be worn on your back. This changes your experience of the game entirely; the gun no longer has weight, and you're not going to run out of air as quickly, but you're running around with air tanks strapped to your back, which some players find annoying.

STEVE DAVIDSON BEING CAUGHT SHORT

"When I started playing in the early 1980s, fields were charging twenty to thirty cents a ball and fifty cents a twelve gram. You were considered a nut if you carried more than about fifty rounds onto the field. Well, I was a nut. I carried a hundred rounds. You see, I got caught short one time. But never again. I'm never going to be stuck out there without ammunition again."

Paintballs

By now it's probably clear that a big part of this game is about splattering paintballs on your opponents. Paintballs come in a variety of sizes: .50, .62 (which is often called, .60), .63, .68, and .72 caliber. .68 caliber paintballs are spherical and dominate the market. The paint substance is

composed of washable, nonflammable, food grade dye. In the early days it was oil based, and players held *de facto* turpentine parties at the end of the day. Not so anymore. Today, regular laundry detergents will do the trick!

Accessories

In most cases, you play a couple of 15 minute paintball games using 1 air tank and topping off your hopper in between sessions. But there will come a time when you'll be playing a significantly longer game, and will need to replenish your supplies on the field. Or, a ball may break in your gun, and you'll need to clean it with a squeegee on the fly. In those moments, you'll be glad you brought the following accessories.

Harness—Usually something worn around the waist that holds extra supplies—extra air, extra paint, maybe even smoke bombs. Typically they are called 4-1 or 8-1 or 6-1. The "1" is usually a vertical receptacle for an air tank. The other numbers signifies spaces for horizontal guppies (tubes for holding paintballs).

Squeegee—An instrument you'll find enormous useful if a paintball explodes in your barrel. This is also useful for the maintenance and upkeep of your gun.

Durty Games

THERE'S MORE THAN ONE WAY TO...

Hi there. Durty Dan here. These games were designed with established fields in mind. That is, the area is all set up, marked out, has flag stations and the like. When writing the rules, I tried not to insult your intelligence by mentioning painfully obvious facts. I figured I didn't have to tell you that the games start and end with a whistle or horn. You will also notice that a lot of rules from the basic Capture the Flag game are repeated in each game, I've done this so you don't have to keep referring back to the original game. Each game stands on its own.

Field owners will find these games an interesting addition to the games they may already run on their field. You may need to adapt the rules to your own particular needs, but remember that safety is always your number one concern.

I purposely did not include games like speedball. (These games and other games requiring structures will already exist where the structures exist on the field.) Not every field will have a speedball course, a village or a fort. The reason for not including these types of games is an attempt on my part to make these games universal. With a little preparation you should be able to play these games on any field in the world.

Speaking of fields, do not confuse "established" fields, with "commercial" fields. Established fields have a playing area already set up to play at least Capture the Flag. Whether it's a "legitimate/commercial" field or a "bootleg/outlaw" field is beside the point.

I have been to some "legitimate/commercial" fields where I was afraid to take off my goggles at any time, unless I was in my car with the windows rolled up. I have also heard of a "bootleg/outlaw" field who sent a guy home for having a hot gun!

Unless otherwise stated, these five rules apply to all the games in this chapter. These are referred to as...

GENERAL RULES

1. All players must begin the game at their flag station (or assigned starting point) and cannot leave that area until the game begins.

2. Players who are hit are out of the game.

3. Players who are eliminated may not, by word or gesture, indicate any intentions or locations of the opposing team members.

4. If a player is eliminated while he is carrying the flag, he must drop the flag where he was hit, or hang it on the nearest available object (not another player).

5. When a player is carrying the flag, it must remain visible at all times and be carried in the hand, over the arm, or around the neck.

–DD

Known as the "World's Most Famous Recreational Player," Durty Dan started his writing career in 1992 when Randy Kamiya (then Editor for *Action Pursuit Games Magazine*) published his first article in the February issue. Since then he has written for *Action Pursuit Games*, *Paintball Sports International* (in his column Rec-Ball), *Paintball Industry Magazine* (no longer in publication), *Paintball News*, *Paintball RAGazine* (no longer in publication), and *Paintball Magazine*.
He has been playing since 1984 and has just recently celebrated his 15th anniversary of playing paintball. Since 1992, he has had an amazing two hundred and fifty articles published, and is in the process of writing a paintball book.

ATTACK AND DEFEND

Requirements
Two teams of equal strength: One team, the Attackers; the other, the Defenders.
Choose a defensible area to serve as a flag station.
Defenders should be restricted to the confines of the flag station.
Set boundaries that limit the movement of the defenders out of the flag station.

Duration
10 minutes.

Rules
Defenders cannot leave the flag station area, or the areas of the flag station they are charged with defending.
The Attackers can attack from any place on the field.
General Rules 1, 2, 3 apply.

Objective
Attackers: Pull the flag off its support (a string, branch, cone, etc.)
Defenders: Stop the Attackers from pulling the flag.

ANNIHILATOR

Requirements
Set up multiple five man teams.
The maximum limit is four teams for every acre of playing area.
Place teams in the area so that they are not in line of sight of each other.
To make score-keeping easier, the teams may be accompanied by a referee and each team may should their own distinct color of paint.

Duration
30–45 minutes

Rules
Teams will stay in their starting stations until the start of the game signal.
Teams get points for each elimination they inflict on other teams.
There are no points for surviving members of the team.
General Rules 1, 2, 3 apply.

Objective
Survive and be the team with the highest score at the end of the game.

Welcome to the Game of Paintball

BLACKJACK

Requirements
Two flag stations
Two even teams
Two flags, hung in opponents' flag stations.
Each player is only allowed 21 paintballs.

Duration
30 minutes

Rules
Players are not allowed to share paintballs.
Players who shoot all of their paintballs must
 leave the game immediately.
All General Rules apply.

Objective
Capture the opposing team's flag and return it to
 your base!

BUNNY HUNT

Requirements
A "Bunny" (one person) and Hunters (everybody
 else).
One player volunteers to be the Bunny. To give the
 Bunny some kind of advantage, choose one of
 these options.
OPTION 1-Give the Bunny a semiautomatic
 paintgun plus a garbage can lid or other device
 to use as a shield.
OPTION 2-Give the Bunny as much paint as he's
 comfortable with, and restrict the Hunters to 20
 paintballs each.

Duration
20 minutes.

Rules
If the Bunny chooses OPTION 1, hits on the shield
 do not count as an elimination.
The Bunny has a 5 minute head start into the
 playing area.
A signal will be given so that the Bunny knows
 when the game is started.
All hunters must start at the same time and from
 the same place.
When using the limited paint option, if a hunter
 runs out of paint, he is out of the game.
General Rules 1, 2, and 3 apply.

Objective
If you're the Bunny, SURVIVAL IS THE GOAL!
If you're a Hunter, eliminate the BUNNY!

who don't understand that and you have to keep pushing them and reminding them. Some people just blank out and start to lift their goggles after a game is over. You just can't do that, and we never let people forget it.

Beyond keeping their eyeballs in their heads, we like our players to feel like they're spending most of their time doing what they came to do. Players are there to get their money's worth. They expect to be moved efficiently through the entire process—get their release forms filled out, get their gun and equipment rentals in hand quickly, buy paint, get to the field. Players should be able to start playing very quickly and play as many games as possible during the course of the day. Sufficient logistics are of primary importance.

To accomplish this, we need a professional staff—motivated, helpful people, who know how to treat customers properly and handle situations

in an appropriate manner. People who enjoy delivering on customer service.

ANDREW: You're doing something right in terms of the way you're conducting your business. People speak very highly of their experience here. Word of mouth is priceless. People tell other people, "I had a great time at Skirmish. They were really nice people, I felt really comfortable, and their fields are

awesome." These are all things that add up to a successful operation.

PAUL: You have to run your field in a professional, businesslike manner. That has been a problem in paintball, but it's improving. For years there were a lot of fields that weren't being run well, but as the sport matures, only the fields that have their act together will survive. Most of the poorly run fields are dropping by the wayside. Not long ago, an insurance guy told me he figured that about forty percent of the fields still didn't have any insurance. That's just ridiculous. Wake up, field-owners. You could lose everything and hurt paintball's reputation in the process!

ANDREW: It seems that to engineer a fun day of paintball, a certain plan is required. Are you guys following a program, whereby teams that start on field "A" will move on to field "B", whereas teams that start on field "Y" go on to field "Z"?

PAUL: No, it's not that scientific. There are large, open fields and small, wooded fields, and fields thick with 15-foot-high rhododendron bushes. We have a general manager, Karen, who evaluates the groups and she puts them on the field where she thinks it's appropriate for that group to start. For example, if it's forty people she puts you on a field that would handle forty people size-wise.

During the course of the day, the judges talk to the players, who are usually pretty forthcoming about what they want. They'll request fields, and we try to accommodate them.

There's one person whose job it is to keep track of who's playing where and they radio in about which fields are open. That person will look at the group and see how many people there are, see what fields they've played, which field is open. You just try and vary it a little bit. You're kind of throwing them a curve, keeping things exciting and new.

I really think the secret to our success is that the fields are a little bit bigger and there's a little bit more anticipation before the shooting starts than in most places. Most places really pack you in.

ON FIELD DESIGN

ANDREW: Who's job is it to design the field?

PAUL: Dewey Green and I are the chief designers. It's a constant tinkering and feedback process. Various judges and players also make suggestions regarding their preferences and desires. Once or twice a year, a group of us will get together over beer and pizza. We brainstorm new field designs and game formats.

THE ROLE OF THE JUDGE

ANDREW: It seems important to have someone on the field who is a representative of the paintball field's operator-the judge. What is a judge?

PAUL: On a recreational level, a judge is a combination of referee and guide. He or she helps the group with their equipment, leads them through the day, and then will make some calls on the field. By the very nature of the fact that you're playing on a number of acres in the woods, the referees cannot make all the calls. There always has to be an honor factor.

The best judges are people with extroverted

personalities, who kind of enjoy the woods. A lot of the judges are there because they like to run around in the woods. I often hear them say things like, "I sit behind the computer terminal all week, so it's fun to get out here and get some exercise."

ON CLOTHING

ANDREW: How should I prepare myself for a day of play? What would you recommend as the proper clothing?

PAUL: Just wear old clothes. If you have a set of fatigues, wear them. Dark colors are a good idea—black, brown, green. Clothes that you will not mind getting wet, dirty, muddy, or splattered with paint.

As an option, most fields offer some sort of camouflage overalls, or "cammies," for rent. You just step into them; they fit over your clothes. At the end of the day, you turn them in and let someone else worry about cleaning them.

Shoes are probably the most important consideration. Go for something light with ankle support and avoid heavy boots.

ANDREW: What about food and water?

PAUL: A good field will provide that stuff for you. Of course, you can bring your own. A good field will have adequate food service and drink. You've got to stay hydrated to avoid cramps and overheating.

WHAT KIND OF GAMES ARE PLAYED

ANDREW: What are the different games you play at Skirmish?

PAUL: There are an infinite variety of games you can play. Center Hang is when you put one flag in the middle of the field and both teams try to get it and take it through to the other team's side of the field. It's like scoring a touchdown. That's a pretty popular game.

The top one is certainly Cap-

Your basic rental gear.

ture the Flag. The second most popular game is probably Center Hang. Number three would be Offense/Defense or Attack and Defend. One team defends their position and the other team just attacks it and they usually have to go in and get the flag or pull it down, or take it out beyond a boundary.

Frankly, the twenty-four hour scenario games are my favorite. They are as interesting as the people who come to play them. We're talking serious paintball hobbyists. In a twenty-four hour scenario game, you've got what seems like unlimited time. So you're not worried about it. And the field of play is huge.

You can go out on a mission and it might take you two hours to try and attain a certain objective. The guy that's directing it, the scenario director, he's just playing with you. He basically sends you out on this mission and then calls up the other coordinators on their radios and he gives them codes that tell them where you're going so that you can be ambushed.

Now, you as a player understand that he's doing this, so you know you have to be careful. Your opponents are going there for the same reason and maybe they've had a half an hour head start on you. Even though you know what's going on, there's still a great deal of suspense.

Sometimes a squad will go out and count how many tents are set up in the enemy's base camp. The players have to try and get that information and bring it back. You earn points if you complete that mission.

Another mission may involve a downed pilot in Sector Five on your map. One of the judges goes out and lays there and makes believe he's the downed pilot. Sometimes they've got to take a stretcher out there, put him on it, and bring him back on it. Very intense stuff.

Whatever the mission, scenario games are highly complex and some people are really into this role playing. Guys come out here with night vision goggles, radios, set up "booby traps" and ambushes. We even have homemade tanks.

We do run three or four scenario games a year, but we only do two twenty-four hour games. The other ones last about eight hours—we call them "mini-scenarios."

ANDREW: How does outdoor paintball differ from indoor paintball?

PAUL: When you play outdoors, the fields are larger and it takes time before "engaging" your opponents. From your position, you can see them coming and you can watch and you can hide and you don't have to move.

Whenever I've played indoors, there's no ambush factors really. You can hide against this wall, but your opponent is still right there . You cannot set an ambush and watch him moving towards you, waiting for the right moment to open fire. Everything happens at a much further distance in the woods, so it's not quite as scary. Indoors can be pretty scary. People are shooting at close range, surprising you from around corners and obstacles.

ANDREW: That's how I experienced it. Indoors does have a frantic intensity. This one place I went to played the Mission Impossible theme before the game. Everybody gets revved up. Add

DEAD MEAT

NICE & TIGHT

LOOKING

In order to stay in the game, new players need to avoid tunnel vision, or the tendency to fixate on one object, one opponent or one activity, to the exclusion of all else.

To avoid tunnel vision, practice shifting your attention among all of the activities in the game in a regular order. Look to your left, look ahead of you, look to your right, check your gun's condition, the paint in your loader, check your rear and your front, and then repeat the procedure.

Eventually you will learn to split your attention properly. You will also learn what you need to pay attention to and what you can ignore. Your main goal during your first few games should be to get a pattern down and then remember to use it.

"WHY IS MY GUN SHOOTING SIDEWAYS?"

This is a simple, yet forgettable, skill. Before you go on the field, make sure that your gun is clean, your goggles are clear, "your tank has enough gas," and you're carrying enough paint for the game.

SELF-ELIMINATION

Too many players lose game-time, and valuable experience, by thinking that because they've run out of paint or air, or their gun goes down, the game is over for them.

You can leave the field if you want to, but why would you want to. Stay and concentrate on learning. Find ways to stay in the game longer. Learn to hide. Learn to crawl. Learn to bluff the other team.

Get as much playing time as you can, regardless of the condition of your equipment.

FAILURE TO REDUCE THE TARGET

Making yourself small is an important skill. The smaller you are, the harder you are to see and to eliminate. In order to 'tuck in' effectively, you have to be aware of exactly where your arms, legs, head, gun, and other equipment are at all times.

This is one of those skills that simply takes time to acquire. However, you can speed up the process by paying attention to where you get hit after the game and by looking at how you take and use cover during the game.

Once in cover, pull your elbows into your body. Tuck your legs in. Get your head down. When you come out of cover to view the field, only expose one eye. While you are shooting, keep your gun barrel as close to the edge of your cover as possible.

Don't use a classic shooter's hold on your gun. Twist the arm of your trigger hand down under the gun. Place the arm of your support hand under the gun as well. When done correctly, both of your elbows should be almost touching on or in front of your chest.

TELEGRAPHING YOUR MOVES

When you break cover, and if you really want to play you're going to have to, you don't want to meet up with a paintball just hanging in the air waiting for you.

Take the precaution of varying where, when, and how you break cover. If your head constantly pops up over the top of a bunker, in the exact same place every time, someone on the field is going to target that spot and keep on shooting at it until you are gone.

To avoid telegraphing, never pop out in the same place two times in a row. Change everything: pop out low on the left, high on the right, from close in on your cover to backed away from your cover. There are thousands of ways you can break cover, and you should be trying to use every one of them.

FAILURE TO USE ANGLES

If you are using cover properly, the last player on the field who is a threat to you is the one directly in front of you. Once you're down behind that bunker or tucked in behind a tree, you can't shoot at the players to your front, and they can't hit you.

This basic situation means that you must shoot to the sides, or at an angle from your cover. Forget about the players in front of you and look for the ones off to the left and the right. Look deep across the field if you are towards the center, or look out to the opposite boundary if you are near the tape. You'll be surprised at how many targets you can find.

LACK OF AGGRESSION

Being aggressive does not necessarily mean running straight down the field hollering your head off. And yet, you might be surprised to learn that this actually works once in a while.

Aggression is a finely balanced thing; too much and you end up in an over-exposed position with the inevitable result. Not enough and you end up making your moves too little, too late.

Pushing the envelope will help you learn just how far you can go. Next time you play, try to get to a piece of cover that is just a little closer to your opponents. And then the next, and the next. Try to get behind them. Try running further down the field at the opening of the game. Push it, and then keep on pushing it. If you see an opportunity to win the game, rally your teammates around you, and make it happen.

A MULTI-DIMENSIONAL GAME

Paintball is not just a stand-up game. It's a kneeling game. A crouching game. A lying game. A crawling game. A timing game.

Being in a particular location on the field at the beginning of the game may be very safe. Towards the end of the game, the same spot might be the last place you would want to be.

If you can't move up the field by running, try crawling. If you are lying behind cover and can't make the shot, try it from a sitting position. If you want to move to another position, wait until no one is looking at you.

Use the entire field, all of the time.

—SD

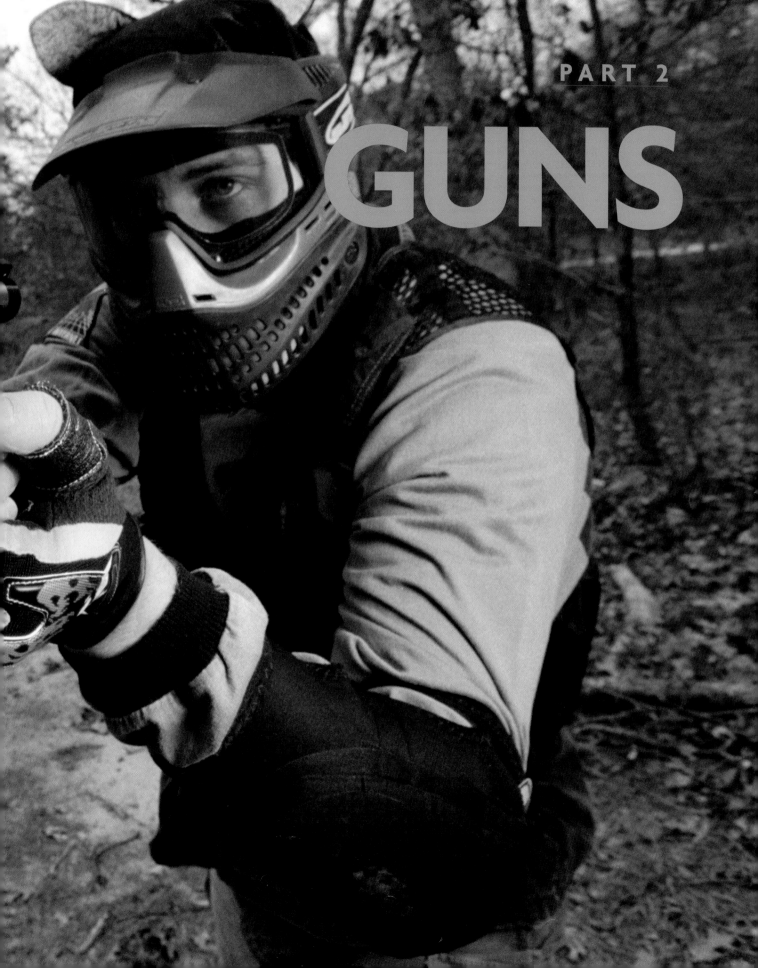

PART 2

GUNS

The Science of Paintball

PAINTBALL 101

Required reading for hard core paintball enthusiasts!

At its inception, paintball borrowed its technology and science from other sources out of sheer necessity. There was no such thing as a 'paintball gun', a paintball designed to be shot at 300 feet per second, paintball specific goggles, or any other piece of specialized equipment, simply because the game did not yet exist. But there was precedent for the development and production of these things, so paintball really hit the ground running.

During paintball's formative years, enterprising individuals and companies developed products using a trial-and-error, cut-and-paste, tinkering-in-the-garage approach. In scientific circles this is known as an 'empirical' method. You come up with an idea, build something based on the idea, identify its flaws and errors by using it, make corrections, add refinements, and continue on to a finished product.

Science, in the form of highly educated and degreed individuals working out complex formulas on blackboards, was not necessary. That work had already been done. The art of creating paintball products and equipment was simple and straightforward. If you could understand how a paintball gun worked, if you could cut PVC tubing with a hacksaw, work a mill or a lathe, or sew a few pieces of material together, you were in business.

There are many other scientific disciplines pushing the paintball we know and love today toward an even more amazing tomorrow. So many, in fact, that it is impossible to cover them all adequately. It is amazing though how rapidly the science of paintball has progressed from a garage-tinkering hobby to the cutting edge of various scientific endeavors.

—SD

JOHN RICE **ON SAFETY**

Paintball has developed extraordinarily fast over a very short period of time. We've come a long way from the traditional little pistol that used to fire one shot and then required a reload. And everyone used to wear a completely unsafe goggle system. Nowadays you're going up eighteen shots plus, and the goggles are designed to withstand the impact of balls traveling 200 miles per hour in rapid succession. It's a whole new standard of safety for a whole new kind of game. As an industry, we've agreed to hold back on firing rates. My technology could take us up to thirty shots per second, but is the player ready for that? Is the safety equipment ready for that intensity? No matter what, safety needs to set the limit for the implementation of new technologies. On that, we should all agree.

Guns

Principles of Worr

Bud Orr

"My dad always said, 'If some guy built it, then you can fix it.'"

In 1953, Bud Orr learned about engine conversions from his father. In 1960, he worked for the U.S. Air Force as a jet fighter mechanic. In 1969, he started working for the Navy overhauling ships (literally, entire ships!). He took up scuba diving, and soon began learning about air flow, gas pressure, and soon began redesigning regulators and compressors. Then, in the mid-1980s, Bud fell in love with paintball, Much of what makes paintball what it is today is directly attributable to innovations pioneered by Bud Orr, founder of Worr Games Products.

ADAM COHEN: So how did you discover paintball?

BUD ORR: Well, one day I came back from vacation and my family wanted to go play paintball. My son wouldn't go unless I went. So, we all went, and basically, I think I rented a PGP at the time and I got shot up pretty bad. And, of course, I loved it.

ADAM: This is back in 1985?

BUD: Yes. And from that point on, we went ahead and went back the next weekend and I thought I could do better because I had thought about the game. The same thing happened, but I figured out why they were shooting at me. Every time I released a CO_2 to change it, they'd run up on me. They were listening carefully and knew when my gun was dead.

So, I went home that week and developed a little device that enabled me to vent CO_2. The following weekend I had more success. I'd vent it, they'd run up, and I'd shoot them. Then, I started modifying guns because I didn't have enough CO_2's. So, I made a manifold so I could actually bolt more CO_2's on it. I was into scuba diving at the time and designed some stuff for the scuba diving industry, so I had access to these little quick release devices. I used them to make it so that you didn't have to expend CO_2 until you pulled a lever.

So, I made a manifold, I bolted two of those on there, and I went out and played all day with two 2.5 ounce CO_2 cylinders.

ADAM: Up to this point, you were doing this primarily because you just loved the game?

BUD: That's right. I just loved it. It was an adrenaline rush. Up to that point... well, I've been a racer all my life. I'm real competitive as far as racing is concerned—drag car racing, sports car racing, boat racing, motorcycles, you name it, I've done it.

The adrenaline rush was just about like it was in racing, only it lasted longer. Just the thrill of the hunt and of being hunted. There's nothing like it, not to this day. Two hours of pure adrenaline rush.

I just started improving the guns. We went to stick feed and then I went over to Sat Cong village and I was a gunsmith there. And in late '86, I was shooting Annihilators. I was actually buying and selling them, and I couldn't really get them from the guy that was making them. He sort of laughed at my ideas for improving the gun. So I went home that week, designed in my head what I wanted to build, and prepared to put it together myself.

Autococker, in all its glory!

There's 10 people playing, and you're against all of them. That's the way to play paintball.

ADAM: That's definitely old-school paintball.

BUD: Yup. That puts a whole new aspect on it. We used to play one on one. We used to play "hare and hound" at Easter time. They'd send a 'hare' running, and then release a 'hound' every 15 seconds. They were all against each other, but the goal was to eliminate the hare. So they're hunting someone who can shoot back at them, and they have to look over their shoulders, because every hunter has incentive to take out the other hunters as well. It was awesome. And I think they still do it like that in some places. But those are just scenarios.

We'd take Easter Day, get 30, 40, 50 people out there, and run two or three games, with everyone fending for himself. There's just not a rush like that. It's unreal.

ADAM: You and Hayes Noel are birds of a feather on this view of the game.

BUD: That guy is incredible.

ADAM: Have you played with him?

BUD: Never played with him, but have you ever met him? That guy is just absolutely top of the line. He's just a really neat, fun, individual. I don't know of anybody that could say anything bad about him. He's put me where I am, and I appreciate that. He just started paintball. I'm one of the people that followed in his footsteps when he backed out of it.

ADAM: If he hadn't played that first survival game...

BUD: ...I wouldn't be in business today.

You know, I had often thought about what he thought about, but I didn't know what to use. I was going to use blow guns or darts or slingshots. I always wanted to see if I could survive in the woods, with people chasing me around.

ADAM: Looks like you got your wish.

BUD: Sure did.

ADAM: I really appreciate your sharing your insights with us.

BUD: No problem.

AUTOCOCKER

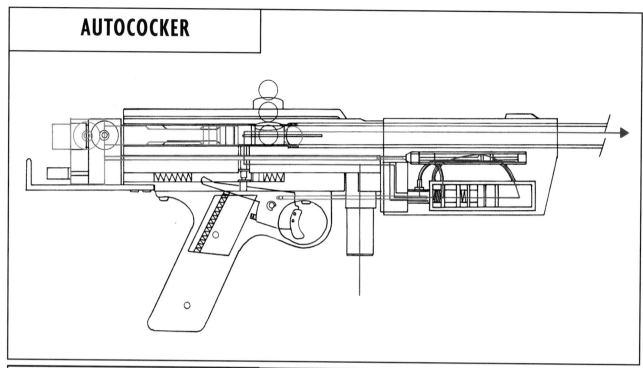

ANGEL

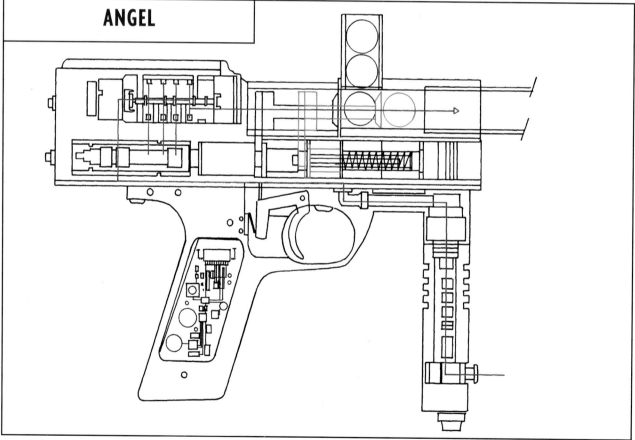

Red lines indicate the action of the bolt.
Blue lines trace the path of the gases.

GUTS

SHOCKER

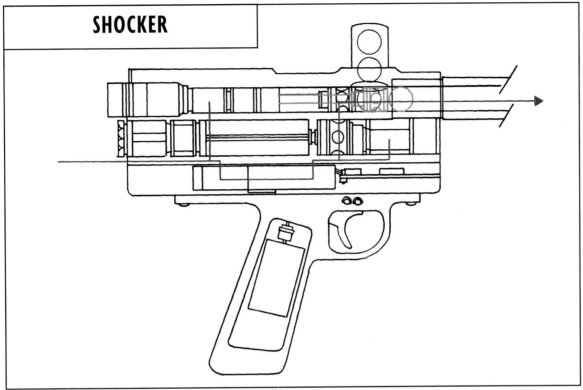

AUTOMAG

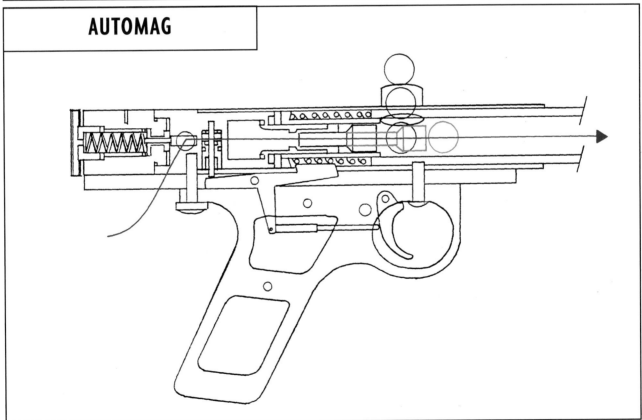

How the Angel Got Its Name and Everything Else You've Always Wanted to Ask This Man

John Rice graduated college with a degree in metallurgy and spent 12 years at TI research laboratories in Cambridge, England, and another 5 years at GE/GEC joint ventures based in England. He specialized in materials technology, high vacuum and surface coating technologies for Joint European Toruss at Harwell Atomic Research. He joined WDP in 1994, working in their new product developments division, and signed on full time as Technical Director in 1995. At 35 years-old, John has been married for 13 years and has a 9 year-old child. His first gun was a Bushmaster, his favorite pump gun is the Sterling, and his first semi-automatic was the Automag.

John Rice and his gun, The Angel, are legendary in the paintball industry. One of the most coveted guns around, the Angel is the first electropneumatic gun to arrive on the scene.

ANDREW FLACH: Where did the idea for the Angel originate?

JOHN RICE: There are certain stars in paintball, players who are very skilled and fast on the trigger. Joe Public wants to be a star. So, I think, how can I make "Joe" a star? The first question in my mind was "how easy is it for 'Joe' to pull a trigger?"

I thought that if I could make it possible for anyone to pull a trigger real fast, as fast as someone who's super fit, it's going to appeal to that player because achieving something awesome will feel "easy."

Now, if you have something that's mechanical and there's a certain timing sequence to maximize the rate of fire, you have to be quite skilled in coordination to achieve the desired result. That's a disadvantage to some players, whereas it might be an advantage to others. So I wanted a leveler, I wanted everybody to have their 15 minutes of fame. That's where electronics come in.

ANDREW: Did you wake up one morning and say 'Eureka'?

JOHN: No, it wasn't as easy as that. If you could have seen the prototype you'd know what I mean. It was spread over about a 5 foot table—bits of valve over here, some electronics over there. Have you ever heard the term "Heath Robinson?"

ANDREW: Heath Robinson is a term? No, I haven't.

JOHN: "Heath Robinson" is English terminology. He was a famous artist who used to draw crazy machines to solve simple problems. Like America's Rube Goldberg. Our first products were like that.

ANDREW: In other words, it did its thing, but you couldn't fit it into a gun.

JOHN: Exactly. But we were thinking about how we were going to make this work. Some of the technology simply wasn't available at the time. That was a major hurdle. I was quite fortunate that, with my background in the industry, I could apply certain industrial technologies to paintball. My former research and engineering experience exposed me to a wide range of possibilities.

New types of materials and different ways of doing things. I realized early on that what I wanted to achieve with a paintball gun could only be achieved with electronics.

I had to take a lot of what the individual did out of their control. I just wanted them to point the gun and pull the trigger, I didn't want them to have to apply any further skill to that process. Basically, that's what the electronics do.

The Angel was born out of my desire, my frustration, my blood, sweat, and tears. And also out of the faith of people like Gerard Green. He believed that we could come up with a product that would work.

We targeted a niche market; the Angel is aimed squarely at the top pro player. It's made in England, and, as I'm sure you've heard, it's very expensive. That's the first thing people say: "It's expensive. Why should I pay that much money?" The answer is that making things in England is expensive. Our labor costs are very high. Machine costs and raw materials are more expensive. These facts, in conjunction with our commitment to R&D and next generation products, plus the level of customer support we offer, lead to an expensive product, but one with a great deal of value built into it. The consumer is receiving the most technically advanced paintball gun in existence.

Europe nowadays cannot rely on a mass market. I don't know if you're aware of how the European market works, but mass marketing in Europe is dead. We can't compete with Poland or Taiwan. So, we specialize. In Europe, everything's moving towards specialization.

ANDREW: Craftsmanship is a way of adding value.

JOHN: Exactly. So we set up the Angel, developed it, launched it, aimed at a very small niche, low production numbers, at the top end player. Due to it's success, it's actually cascaded down, which has surprised us. We're amazed at how many Angels we've sold. And we're actually seeing young kids buying them. 12-year-olds are hassling their parents to buy them. And yes, we'll build a rapport with the parents, offer them support. But that's amazed us.

Our product was not targeted at them. And you know, when you see a young lad come up to you, 12 years old, and he's holding his Angel up, it does knock you for six a bit. [*Laughs*]

One thing we recognized very quickly was that our product was moving across the pond, and to support customers we had to come to America on a regular basis. Because if you're asking someone to part with a lot of money and they say, "I've got a problem, where do I go?", you better be able to answer them.

ANDREW: So, what year marked the origin of the Angel?

JOHN: The first working prototypes that you could actually hold in your hand and play with appeared in 1995. That's when you could actually say "this gun looks like an Angel."

ANDREW: Who named it?

JOHN: Dave Poxon, our Marketing Director. Have you ever heard of a rock group called Saxon? It's a heavy metal group, early 80s, and he used to be its manager. He was into marketing, and he knew which way the music industry was going. He said "Angel is going to be a big word on the music scene," and he chose it as the name of our gun, too. Sure enough, records come out with "angel" themes and lyrics, and it became this new happening thing. That's his skill.

That's how the Angel name came about. It was called the Angel V6. We chose V6 because it sounds gutsy, earthy. In America they like V6. It was V6 because it's 6 volt, no other reason. Amazingly, we dropped the V6, but people over here still say, "Oh, I've got a V6."

Also, the Angel had another appeal. It's a little mysterious. A little sinister. A

little dangerous. You could turn a dark side to it. That's where the Dark Angel was born.

ANDREW: Double entendre.

JOHN: That's it. And it worked very well for us. So that's how the Angel got its name.

Another interesting bit of Angel trivia is the fact that on the packaging, the gun depicted is a left-handed model. The reason it is photographed this way is because I'm left-handed. It wasn't until very late into the design and production of the Angel that we spotted the oversight.

Andrew: So the early production models, the design models...

JOHN: ... are all left handed.

ANDREW: What is it that makes the Angel a unique paintball gun for the player?

JOHN: First of all, the shape works well. It's very sleek, very modern looking. That's come out of European styling more than American styling. In America, space is so free. Everything in the U.S.A. is big. Look at your appliances, look at your cars, look at your houses. You've got space, and you like to fill it. The Americans also like to bolt things on and add things because of this perception that there is no space restriction. In Europe, everything's got to be small. We made everything small deliberately.

People buy instant prestige when they buy an Angel. They're buying something that is European, that is new, that is unique.

Andrew: Tell us about the Angel's technical features.

JOHN: With the Angel, you can have a very short trigger pull. In fact, the first prototype triggers were so soft you could literally blow on them and they would go bang. People shot themselves a good deal. [*Laughs*]

So the trigger is very easy to use, everybody can pick up an Angel and achieve a very high rate of fire. They don't need the skill to do it.

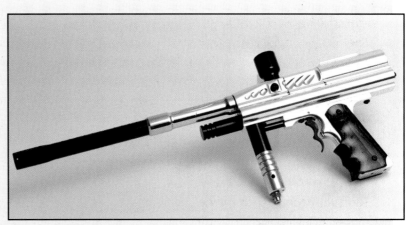

Manufacturer: Warped Sports **Type:** Dark Angel **Description:** Customized and modified Angel with double trigger. *Courtesy of Rocky Cagnoni.*

ANDREW: Now, when you pull the trigger you're activating a circuit?

JOHN: You're basically starting a sequence of events.

ANDREW: What is the sequence?

JOHN: The sequence of events is basically as follows. When I pull the trigger, I start an elaborate clock which now needs to drive electro-pneumatic valves and solenoid valves. And what we've actually got is a Japanese valve. We call it a "fourteen way valve."

It's called that because it has fourteen gas galleries. It's a very reliable valve. The Japanese have done an excellent job in miniaturizing it for me. What that then drives is a traditional mechanism, and although there are several unique features that we've patented in that mechanism, it's still using gas to fire a paintball.

Gas comes into the fourteen way valve and it drives a servo. A servo is how to get some movement using less force, like your brake servo on a car. If you didn't have a servo, you'd be pressing on that brake with all your strength to get an effect. The servo translates a mild force into a heavier force.

For example, if I have a very small piston, I could lift a 300 ton weight with my thumb. I'd only move it very slightly, but I could do it, because I could apply force over a very small area, the way a car jack works. It's mechanical advantage. That's what a servo does. A servo actually drives what we call the spool.

The spool changes gas direction, which drives a hammer forward, and that hammer will strike a valve. Just how long that valve is open for is controlled electronically. Controlling it electronically is extraordinarily efficient. This is all happening in sixteen milliseconds. Sixteen thousandths of a second! This eliminates the "chopping of paint."

ANDREW: And chopping paint is?

JOHN: It's where your bolt or your mechanism comes forward, and it literally chops the paintball in half, before it's properly positioned for firing. You can make guns shoot incredibly fast, but you haven't got a hope in hell of shooting paint. Because if a gun's shooting faster than you can feed it paintballs, it turns into an emulsion gun.

ANDREW: You're blasting out broken paintballs.

JOHN: So with the Angel what you can do is actually adjust the timing. Now, because I can control the timing of the firing mechanism through electronics, I can achieve a very high rate of fire. The Angel has the fastest rate of fire of any paintball gun available.

ANDREW: Which is?

JOHN: Currently we've kept it at 13 shots a second, but 18 shots per second capability is built into every Angel. And yes, it will shoot at that rate for those who have discovered it.

ANDREW: Semi-auto or full auto?

JOHN: Either. There's a set of dip switches on a chip inside the gun that changes the mode of firing. You have semi-auto, full auto, three shot burst, and a "zipper burst."

ANDREW: What is a zipper burst?

JOHN: Zipper burst was developed in reaction to what they called the "Turbo Trigger." Essentially, it's an eight round burst. It's purpose was to show the

Wire synchronizes electronic loader with firing rate of the gun.

farcical nature of some of the current definitions of a trigger action. But that's another story altogether.

ANDREW: Would you have specific loader systems that are recommended for use with this or do people widely use whatever they desire?

JOHN: The most popular system is made by Viewloader. It's a motorized system. However, the paintball industry is on the verge of the next big step, which is force feed.

The limiting factor with any of the current loader systems is gravity. Once you take gravity out of it, rate of fire can go sky high. Way above 30, even hundreds of paintballs a second. It's virtually unlimited, in theory.

THE AIR SYSTEM

ANDREW: The Angel is a compressed air gun, right?

JOHN: Correct. Carbon dioxide is a very harsh gas, and the trouble is it's stored in its liquid state. As it turns into gas, its temperature drops. The colder it gets, the less it wants to give off gas. I call CO_2 a "dirty" gas because it's slow to fill up, it freezes, it's not very temperature stable, and it's very abrasive. The ice crystals that form in it are actually physically abrasive to gun parts.

For running a paintball field, CO_2 is attractive. It's cheap, it's simple, because all you're buying are cylinders of CO_2, you don't have to have a high pressure air regulation system.

With the classic 12 ounce cylinder, you can get 2000 shots off under perfect conditions. Such are the thermodynamics of CO_2. That means you fire one shot, you allow the gas pressure and the temperature to recover, and then fire your next shot. Paintball guns aren't used that way, of course. Paintball guns are shooting faster and faster.

ANDREW: So, in other words, the CO_2 has a lag time between shots caused by the nature of the gas.

JOHN: Yes.

ANDREW: Because each shot costs pressure, and it takes time to get back up to pressure.

JOHN: Up to pressure and temperature. So you can take a CO_2 gun and fire it. The number of shots you get out is phenomenal initially, but things go downhill from there.

ANDREW: So compressed air was your vision from the start.

JOHN: Yes. That was the only choice, in my view. I wanted air, nitrogen. I did not want CO_2.

ANDREW: Now, I heard you use a term earlier, low pressure regulator? The LPR. That sounds like a scuba diving term.

JOHN: Because the Angel is pneumatically driven, I need a lower pressure to drive my pneumatics. My servo valve will not survive high pressure, so I needed a lower pressure to do that.

ANDREW: So you need something to stage it down.

JOHN: Correct. The LPR.

THE INFINITY BARREL

ANDREW: What kind of barrel systems do you use? Do you develop your own?

JOHN: We make our own barrels, which we call the Infinity Series. Barrels are such a personal choice. I could sit here and say Infinity barrels are the best barrel in the world and believe it. But in the end, it's very personal.

ANDREW: What are the unique features of the Infinity barrel?

JOHN: It's a step bore. Have you heard of step boring barrels?

ANDREW: No, tell me what that means.

JOHN: Step boring a barrel is an old system in the manufacture of real firearms for many years. Basically it's a barrel with two bores, each with a separate diameter. The smaller bore provides the acceleration and the wider bore provides guidance. The holes in the side provide a silencing effect.

Now, previously everybody's accomplished this step bore manufacturing process in a two part design. Our two bores are achieved with one tool. Traditionally, step boring required people to hone a bore of one diameter in the first tube, and another diameter in a second tube. Then the two tubes would have to be mechanically joined.

We actually achieve two bores with the same equipment. If you look down the barrel, you can actually see the two bores. Hold it at a distance, and you'll see something like a ring. That's where the two bore diameters meet. No seam is visible.

We don't hone. Some people hone barrels out, we don't. We use a technology that was developed in Germany, using special types of tools and special high pressure coolants. It gives us an edge that no one else has. I believed it was the best way to go. I don't have any misalignment problems involved with joining two points together.

THE LED DISPLAY AND THE FUTURE OF ELECTROPNEUMATIC GUNS

ANDREW: I notice there's a LED on the back of the Angel? What information does that give the player?

JOHN: Looks good, doesn't it?

ANDREW: Yeah.

JOHN: A cosmetic thing. Seriously, though, it's a safety feature. Somebody can see it from a distance and know the gun is on and capable of firing. It's a visual indication, too. When you pull the trigger, the LED changes color. The gun makes a bang sound, but it allows you to see that information.

ANDREW: Have you ever thought of putting a counter on the Angel?

JOHN: No comment. But, if you're asking me where paintball's going, I'll tell you where I think it's going. Electronics are here to stay. You're going to be hooking them up to your computers, you're going to have digital displays. You're going to have RS232 ports, infrared links. You're going to have user interfaces, you're going to have head up displays. That's where the sport's going.

ANDREW: High tech all the way.

JOHN: Technology is being applied to everything. People are timid about electronics initially. When we first launched the Angel, people said "Oh, it's going to be unreliable," or, "It's not going to work." There was a lot of negative speech about electronics. Electronics are used in every walk of life. Anything you do counts on electronics. That's a trend that's only going to get bigger. And soon, any competitive paintball gun will be electronic as well.

ANDREW: What's the next step for WDP? How long is this version of the Angel going to be around?

JOHN: No comment. *[Smiling]*

ANDREW: Why are you smiling?

JOHN: I could tell you, but then I'd have to kill you.

ANDREW: *[Laughs]*

JOHN: Just wait and see.

F/A THE DAY AWAY

Single-Action. Auto-Trigger. Pump-Action. Double-Action. Semiautomatic. Full-Automatic.

Paintball guns have evolved radically over the past eighteen years, driven by players' fervent desire for ever increasing rates of fire. This has become a source of contention, concern, and debate among members of the paintball community.

Back in 1981 and 1982, when this great game was just getting started, there were really only two gun choices: the side-cocking Nelspot, remembered by its users for the calluses it left on their fingers, and the rear-cocking Sheridan PGP. Both guns had to be recocked between shots using a rather complicated procedure. For the Sheridan, you had to turn the bolt a quarter turn, pull it back until it clicked, tilt the gun back, so the ball could roll into the chamber, tilt the gun forward, push the bolt back in, and then turn it back a quarter turn. For the Nelspot, you had to raise the cocking lever, pull it back, tilt the gun forward, tilt it back, push the lever forward, and then lock it in place.

It's hard to remember the procedures in correct order, let alone retain the mindset necessary to shoot someone two or three times using it! It's no wonder that players were considered to be paint hogs when they carried more than 50 or 60 rounds per game.

Rate of fire was not something that concerned those who played the game in its infancy. Waiting an hour for a single elimination was common. Forcing opponents to surrender was considered the highlight of the game. But then, what more can you hope for when you can only fire about three rounds per minute?

Missed shots, chopped balls, empty firing chambers, and general frustration led many players to concoct their own solutions to the problem, beginning with the pump. A relatively simply modification, the pump did away with the need to pull and turn the bolt. Shortly after, someone came up with the idea of the 'gravity feed,' which meant that it was no longer necessary to roll the ball into the chamber. Both ideas were combined and the paintball technological revolution was underway.

The new ideas caught on quickly; less complicated guns meant more people could play the game. More paint being fired meant that game site owners were making bigger profits. Start-up manu-

facturers now had hundreds of potential products and a new audience waiting for them.

Players quickly became obsessed with how many balls they could fire per second. One player remembered his/her course in basic firearms, shaved a gun sear, and created the auto-trigger, a device that eliminated the need to pull the trigger when firing. Your average player, someone who owned their own gun and played regularly, could now pump out four to five rounds per second. Legendary players were clocked at seven rounds per second!

The quest for a user-friendly gun now turned into a mania for increasing rates of fire. Before anyone could figure out how to make a semi-automatic, at least two companies marketed a double-action, the first pumpless paintball gun.

Unfortunately, the mechanics of a double-action (releasing the sear and resetting the bolt in one pull of the trigger) created a slower rate of fire, relegating these guns to the backwater of paintball technology. However, the first generation of semi-automatics was not long in coming.

First introduced around 1990, most new semi-automatics were technological disasters. They were prone to breakdowns and leaks, in addition to being poorly designed and sensitive to weather conditions. Manufacturers were rushing to supply a new demand.

The first protest against this increasing rate of fire made itself heard around this time. Probably due more to the bad performance of the new guns than to anything else, many tournament teams refused to use semiautomatics and lobbied tournament promoters to ban their use also.

This protest was short-lived with the arrival of the second generation of semiautomatics. They were more reliable, less complicated, and backed by some of the most respected companies in the industry. Seeing a trend in the making, many event producers offered 'open class' competition where any gun was welcome. High profile teams began

4. Use an Allen wrench to remove the Max-Flow cradle, which is held in place with two Allen bolts. Use a little elbow grease if needed.

5. You will notice there are two suction connections with o-rings.

6. Remove the Max-Flow regulator.

7. Now we begin removing the bolt assembly. In a counterclockwise motion, twist the knob on the back of the gun that retains the bolt cylinder.

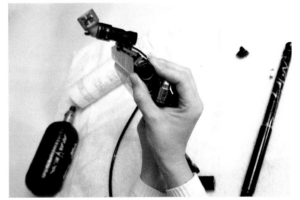

8. Remove the bolt assembly by pulling it out. This is the bolt that pushes the ball out of the gun. Lay it aside for later cleaning.

9. Use a chamois squeegee to clean the barrel housing.

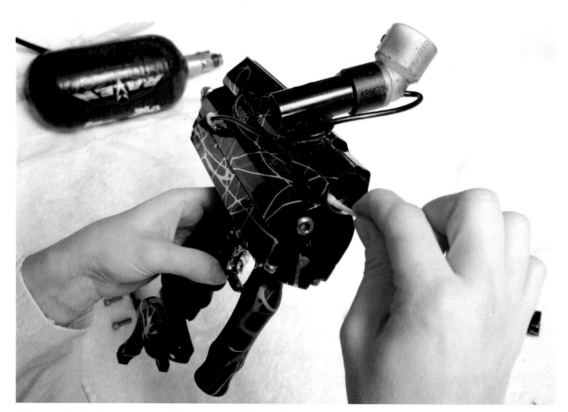

10. Use alcohol impregnated cotton swabs to thoroughly clean the barrel housing area. Any dirt or debris left behind can cause the gun to malfunction.

11. Clean the feeder tube assembly with your chamois squeegee.

12. Clean the Powerfeed plug by wiping it down with a rag.

13. Clean the barrel with the squeegee.

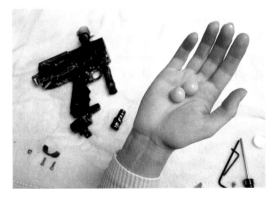

14. Here's a very real reminder about why you should not work on your gun with the air supply attached. During this cleaning, we found two balls still in the system!

15. Now let's turn our attention to the regulator. First, wipe off the excess dirt.

16. Follow that with a more detailed cleaning using cotton swabs and alcohol. Note that dirt is everywhere, including threads, openings, and crevices. Care should be taken to remove it all.

17. Carefully remove grains of dirt from the suction assembly by using an awl. Also use the awl to remove dirt from the cradle.

18. Using the Phillips screwdriver, remove the grip. Since this is an early model, we need to access the battery compartment to disconnect the batteries. Newer Shocker models feature an on/off switch.

19. Disconnect the batteries by pulling apart the connection. Do not grip the wires when disconnecting the battery. Only grip the connectors!

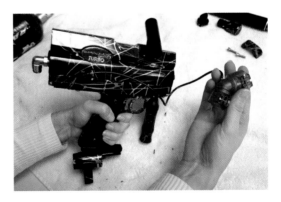

20. Replace the battery in the housing, leaving the wires disconnected. (Remember to reconnect the battery next time you want to play!)

21. Remove the air assist elbow. The air assist applies gentle air pressure to keep the paintballs moving down the elbow into the breech.

Guns

22. Wipe down the gun from top to bottom,

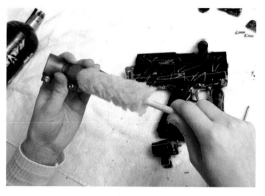

23. Clean the air assist elbow with your squeegee.

24. With cotton swabs and alcohol, clean the threads and seating area where the air tank attaches to the Max-Flow system.

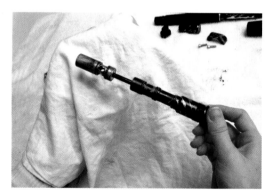

25. Wipe down the bolt. Remove all old lube and dirt.

26. Use a dental pick to clean the holes in the bolt. Get the old lube out before applying new lubricant.

27. The opening at the end of the bolt can get jammed full of paint and broken balls every time you push your squeegee down the barrel to clear a jam. Make sure you clean it out well.

28. Apply a small amount of Dow Corning 33 Silicone Grease to your finger tips and then spread the lubricant throughout the bolt assembly. Movement of the bolt should be free and smooth.

ALMOST THERE...

29. Take care to lubricate all areas where parts of the gun come together—especially o-rings and metal-to-metal contact areas. The lubrication will help make the Shocker easier to disassemble next time.

30. The disassembled Shocker with maintenance and cleaning equipment.

—SS

Choosing a Barrel

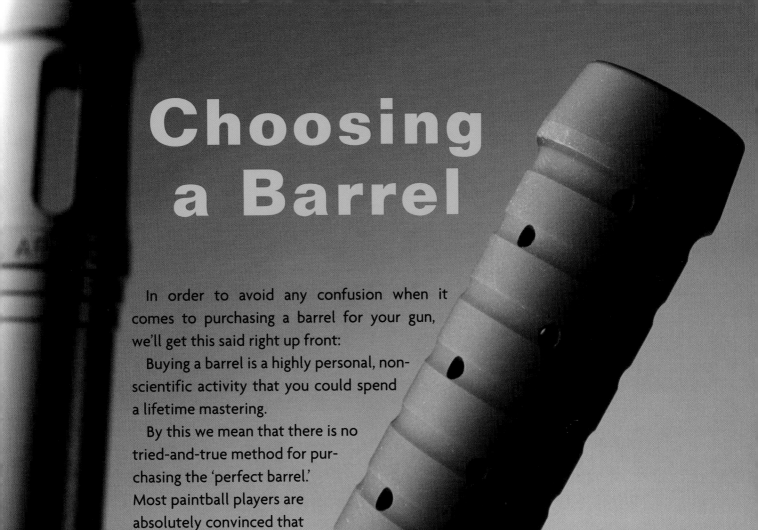

In order to avoid any confusion when it comes to purchasing a barrel for your gun, we'll get this said right up front:

Buying a barrel is a highly personal, non-scientific activity that you could spend a lifetime mastering.

By this we mean that there is no tried-and-true method for purchasing the 'perfect barrel.' Most paintball players are absolutely convinced that they already have the perfect barrel—namely, the one screwed into their gun when they buy it. If this were true, if each gun came packaged with the perfect barrel, then there would be no need to purchase an aftermarket one. That brings us to the critical question:

Is there a need to purchase an aftermarket barrel? The answer is yes... and no.

Most guns are purchased with a 'stock' barrel. Originally, the 'stock' barrel was all you could get. Most gun manufacturers made and continue to make fine barrels. However, once removable barrels arrived on the scene, which not only promised superior performance but were definitely far easier to clean, somebody was bound to make an aftermarket barrel that actually was 'better.' Major growth of demand for aftermarket barrels soon followed. As a result, most gun manufacturers have stopped making expensive stock barrels and instead provide a basic one for you to use until you can go out and purchase a 'perfect' one. Today, there are at least twenty (if not 40) different barrel brands.

But it doesn't stop there. Each brand of barrel has to have a different model for each different gun on the market. Add to this the fact that there is no industry standard when it comes to the manner in which a barrel is attached to a gun, and you have a huge number of barrels available across a wide range of prices. Most are threaded (like a screw), but there are several models which use a 'twist-lock', and several which use a pressure fit.

Barrel Length Counts

Most everyone agrees that you need at least 8 inches of barrel to make the most effective use of the gas and to give the ball some accuracy over decent ranges. After that there is virtually no agreement. Barrels come in lengths ranging from 8 to 18 inches. The length of a barrel also affects the issues of gas volume and pressure: guns with very low operating pressures will require a longer barrel.

Barrels are also made out of several different materials. Aluminum, brass and stainless steel are the most common, but you also can find carbon-fiber barrels and mixed-material barrels. Different inner-coatings also have been added (teflon, for instance), as have various forms of rifling. Barrels can come with 'muzzle breaks,' spiral rifling, gas porting, and a whole museum's worth of external patterns, sculpturing, and colors.

The barrel's inner diameter also varies. This might not seem to make sense. After all, a paintball is .68 caliber, right? Well, in fact, that's not entirely true. The *ideal* paintball is perfectly round and exactly .68 inches in diameter, no matter where you measure it. A real paintball is anywhere from .65 to .70 inches in diameter, sometimes oblong in shape, with a seam around it. In other words, it's far from a true sphere. Paintballs are commonly referred to as small-bore (.65 to .67) and

big bore (.68 to .70). Because of this, the inner diameter (or ID) of a barrel can vary from as small as .685 to .692. Admittedly, this is a relatively small difference—but when it comes to performance, it's a critical one.

Every paintball barrel manufacturer out there will say that the most important factor in choosing a good barrel is picking the right paint. After that, they'll say that the 'fit' between your barrel and the paint you are shooting is the next most important thing. They're right.

Of course, there are the ambient or 'local' conditions, things such as temperature, humidity and air pressure, that also affect performance: the barrel you use today with such amazing results may

belong in the bottom of your gear bag tomorrow, even if you are shooting the same gun, with the same paint at the same velocities as the previous day. The differences in performance may be due entirely to the changing play conditions, and they aren't necessarily your barrel's fault.

No one who plays paintball for any length of time always shoots exactly the same paint each and every game. Paint varies from brand to brand

(and from batch to batch). In order to counter this, most serious rec players have adopted the strategy of collecting a variety of barrels, in different lengths, with different IDs, made out of different materials, so that no matter what paint they are shooting, they will always have a barrel that makes a good match.

The general rules of thumb when buying a barrel relate to the ID, the length, the material it is made from, the presence or absence of rifling, porting and breaking, and the barrel's aesthetics.

Fortunately, you can be a little more discriminating (although you will probably end up with your own barrel bag eventually). When it comes to ID, most companies tend to make one to three different 'bores' (the tube inside the barrel is the bore). These bores generally correspond to a 'tight', a 'medium,' and a 'loose' fit. Tight bores are for small bore paint, loose bores are for big-bore paints and medium bores are for everything in between. Brands that only offer one or two bore sizes usually make a tight and a medium, since most paint tends to be small these days.

Try and settle on a particular brand of paint to use most of the time. This might be a brand offered by a local retailer, the brand of paint sold at your local field, or the paint recommended by local experts. Find out what 'size' this paint is (call the supplier if you have to). Your general-purpose barrel should have an ID which matches this brand of paint, since this is what you will be shooting most frequently.

Material really has only one determining factor, and that is its weight. The lightest barrels are generally 'composites' (carbon fiber) and aluminum, although some companies are doing amazing things with stainless steel. Brass is next in weight, followed by most stainless steel barrels. (Don't forget that the length of a barrel also contributes to its weight.) The smoothness of a barrel's bore is an important factor. The smoother it is, the less friction will be experienced by the ball as it travels through the barrel. All of the materials mentioned have roughly the same smoothness factor, so this is not a huge consideration. Sometimes smoother surfaces actually create greater drag. This is exactly why choosing a barrel is an art, rather than a science.

When it comes to porting, breaking and rifling, it's probably anybody's guess as to which implementation creates the best range or accuracy. Rifling is a technique borrowed from firearms technology. A helix of ridges and grooves is cut down the length of the inner surface of the barrel. These are used to grab the soft body of a bullet and cause it to spin. This gives the bullet greater stability in flight. Unfortunately, paintballs are not solid, aerodynamically shaped objects, and conventional rifling can't be used because it would rip and shatter the paintball. Nevertheless, barrel makers have come up with at least three paintball versions of the same thing, none of which work by 'spinning' the ball, but which can aid it in other ways. Polygonal Progressive Rifling (Armson) barrels have twenty-eight blunt-edged lands (the ridges of rifling) which curve down the inner surface of the barrel. These provide a greater surface area for the ball to seal against and help stabilize the ball as it leaves the barrel. Spiral Porting (Smart Parts) uses a patented external version of rifling. Two lines of 'ports' (holes drilled through the body of the barrel) are created down the length of the barrel in a spiral. This relieves pressure behind and in front of the ball and allows the ball to make a smooth transition to the air. Straight Rifling (J&J) uses four straight lands cut down the length of the bore to provide greater stability and better control of the ball as it moves through the barrel.

Most barrels, however, are 'smoothbore' barrels; they have no rifling of any kind. By the way, players have had tremendous success with all bore styles.

Guns

Muzzle Breaks are another adaptation from 'real guns.' They are typically used to suppress noise, reduce pressure at the muzzle (when the gun is fired), and suppress the 'flash' coming from a barrel. In paintball guns, it is generally believed that a muzzle break will aid the ball when it makes the transition from the barrel to still air. Muzzle breaks can be found on a wide variety of barrels.

Porting is generally used for its sound-suppressing qualities. Small holes (of varying number and size) are drilled down the length, or a portion of the length, of a barrel. These are not cut in a spiral (like the external rifling), but in straight lines. Sometimes slots are used instead of round holes.

And now we come to length. Determining the ideal length for a barrel is the biggest source of controversy when it comes to barrels. Some people swear by long barrels, some by short ones. Some are convinced that thirteen inches is what you need, while others think that sixteen inches is the mandatory minimum. The truth is that only a gun's manufacturer (or someone who works closely with a particular model) knows what the 'best' barrel length for that gun is. In general, you need the length of a barrel for two things.

- First, it needs to be long enough so that an optimal amount of gas will get the ball up to the desired velocity.

- Second, it should be long enough to give the ball some accuracy in its flight. However, if a barrel is too long, it will slow the ball back down again.

Unfortunately, these factors vary from gun to gun. The most efficient barrel, in terms of gas use, is one that is exactly long enough, and no longer. This may not be the same length as is required for the desired degree of accuracy, so choosing a length becomes the art of balancing these two goals within a range that is good for that particular gun.

Usually, an inch or two in either direction won't make a tremendous difference: if your gun 'needs' a twelve inch barrel, you'll still get good performance out of a ten inch barrel or a fourteen inch one.

The basic rule of thumb regarding length seems to be that if you are planning on playing up-front and personal (close to the other team), you want a shorter barrel so that you can 'tuck in'; and it will give you the kind of accuracy you are looking for with short to medium ranges. If you are planning on longballing (shooting long distance), you'll want a longer barrel to increase your sight radius and achieve greater accuracy. Remember to keep in mind that these are relative lengths, based on the kind of gun you are shooting.

A barrel's look is nearly as important as everything that has gone before. If your barrel looks cool, then you look cool, and it hardly matters whether you're hitting anything or not! WOOO-HOOO! (Just kidding.)

Most barrel manufacturers have developed distinctive styles for the outer surface of their barrels. Grooves, cuts, slashes, stippling, bumps and ridges have all been cut into barrels. Then there's color; you can get a barrel in just about any color you can imagine. Other manufacturers have begun to add graphics to their barrels and feature things like flames and skulls. Your typical macho-stuff can be found in virtually infinite variety from the tasteful to the tasteless. Chances are, whatever look you want, you'll be able to find a barrel to match it.

When you finally do go to purchase a barrel, remember to take along the information you've gathered about the kind of gun you are using and the paint you'll be shooting, remember that no barrel lasts forever. Think of your first barrel purchase as the beginning of a long and rewarding learning process, and save up your money so that you can afford to buy the next best thing.

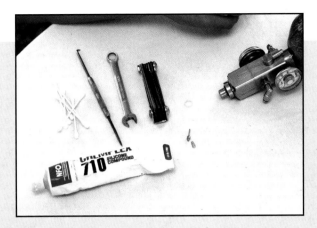

have the knowledge base. So, you'll see them putting black rubber o-rings in there which may last for one cycling of the gun and then blow apart, or they wrap teflon tape around internal portions of the regulator. They're thinking, "Hey, it stopped leaking, so it must work, right? Wrong. That's why a step-by-step process like this is really important. Our air system is very easy to maintain. We try to educate our customers. They get an operator's manual that outlines these same procedures, how to troubleshoot.

STEW: For the basic servicing of the Air America system here, what tools do you need to have?

RON: The main tools you need to do any consumer level maintenance would be a set of hex keys, a main set of 16ths, 5/32nds, a pick or o-ring tool, and a 7/16ths open-end wrench. That'll perform 99% of the maintenance. Q-tip swabs and some rubbing alcohol to clean out dirt and debris, and a lubricating oil or grease.

STEW: Any one in particular for lubrication that you recommend?

RON: What shouldn't you use? A lot of players use vaseline, or auto grease on the piston. Any kind of grease other than this silicone lube I'm using collects dirt. Lightweight motor oil will work fine, as well as gun oil. Any of these can be used to perform routine maintenance and lubrication. In addition to the piston, we also put oil on the mainspring, also called the spring pack. It's a series of stacked concave disks that doesn't look much like a spring, but the concave disks working against each other provides a spring

action. If you don't keep it lubricated, and the disks become corroded, it increases friction and the spring becomes less effective or erratic, and pressure adjustment becomes difficult. So we put a light coat of oil on that spring, which I'll show you when we take it apart, and a light coat of oil on the piston o-ring.

STEW: So you can use petroleum products to lubricate it?

RON: We'd rather the consumer use a ure-thane-friendly lubricant, a non-penetrating type of lubricant. Over time, the o-ring will become hard or swell and tear if they use distillate-type lubricants. This silicone compound we just started using is an industry standard o-ring lubricant. We find that it works very well. But it's not readily available to all of our consumers. So I recommend a light lubricating oil, friendly for ure-thane products.

AIR VS. CO$_2$

STEW: So why air and not carbon dioxide?

RON: Carbon dioxide is a compressed liquid gas. It's more unstable than air and very susceptible to temperature changes. Since it's a liquid, we have a problem. Even with an anti-siphon tube, when a player tilts his bottle down, he is going to get some liquid up into the hose that can cause the gun to freeze up. At a minimum, you'll get hot shots in excess of 300 feet per second, which can be potentially hazardous. With the anti-siphon bottles of today, the technology has advanced to the point where it is safer, but there are still problems. There are always temperature fluctuations. Not to say that CO$_2$ is a bad way to do things, you just have to be aware of how it works. The majority of the entry level paintball guns and field owners still use compressed CO$_2$ because it's more affordable at this point. Due to the materials and labor that are involved, our compressed air systems are a lot more expensive than buying mass-manufactured 12-ounce or 20-ounce CO_2 bottles, which you can pick up for 40 or 50 bucks, depending on the size of the bottle.

STEW: Does it help with cyclical rates of fire? Remember we were talking about using the Shockers and the Angels. They wouldn't use carbon dioxide, would they?

RON: A low-pressure gun needs more volume. Volume is a big deal. One player in a 10-man competition, two 5-man teams going at it, can go through up to 2500 rounds in one game.

The guns vary. Take an Autococker, for example. There are so many after-market products that change the flow dynamics and the volume characteristics that are available for that gun. The average shot count for an Autococker with a 4500 psi system may be 1600–1800 shots per fill. Variations in barrels and different types of actuating mechanisms will affect performance. Different manufac-

turers recommend different volumes. So, we say the average is probably about 1800 shots for this system here. But when you get into a Shocker, with its high-rate of fire and particular volumetric efficiency, it's not going to work for a player who wants to shoot 1800–2,000 rounds. That type of gun typically eats more air than others.

STEW: What do they use to get the volume they want?

RON: They use CO_2. We can use this same type of bottle with a CO_2 valve. The threads are standard. So they can get more with the CO_2 in this same sized bottle than you would with compressed air. There's a trade-off, because now you're carrying around 30 ounces of CO_2 in a heavy bottle. We looked at that added weight, at the risk level involved with carrying that around, and went with compressed air.

DISASSEMBLY AND BASIC MAINTENANCE OF THE REGULATOR

1. The first step in disassembling the regulator is to remove the locked tournament cap that holds the regulator adjustment nut in place.

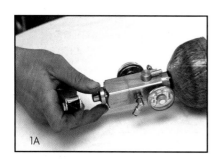

1A

1B

STEW: Can you describe the relationship between the regulator adjustment nut and the tournament cap?

RON: By turning the regulator nut with a hex key, the outgoing pressure is increased by turning it in a clockwise motion and decreased by going counter-clockwise. The tournament cap is locked down, so when the system is not under pressure, the regulator nut does not move. It's called a tournament cap because without it, you would be able to adjust the regulator pressure during the game and increase the speed. This would allow you to get further down the field, but you'd be shooting at other players with a hot gun, so it became a standard rule within the NPPL to have a locking tournament cap on your air system. With the locking cap, you won't be able to increase your pressure on the field and then leave it with a lower pressure.

STEW: How does being able to adjust the pressure affect the gun's performance?

RON: Each gun operates at a different pressure which affects performance. By adjusting the pressure, you're modifying it for that type of gun. Automatic style requires 600–900 psi to operate, depending on what type of valve work has been done to the gun. Standard Autocockers require anywhere from 375–500 psi to operate. This allows you to adjust the air system to whatever inbound pressure your gun requires.

STEW: And then the tournament cap locks that setting?

RON: The tournament cap locks that setting down, so when the air system is de-gassed, there's pressure on the adjustment nut. At that point, when you have to empty your tank, or it is loose in your gear bag, the nut won't float around and change the pressure setting.

2. The second step is to remove the regulator adjustment nut. As we remove it, the mainspring (the spring pack) comes out with it.

2A

2B

3A

3. Remove the mainspring from the regulator nut. Remove the piston from the piston bore.

Stew: Can regular players do all of this? Ron: Yes.

3B

4. Inspect the mainspring for tightness in the disks, corrosion, and check the lubrication.

4

5. Check the o-ring on the piston for any obvious nicks, cuts, scratches, discoloration, water saturation, or swelling. Replace the o-ring if necessary.

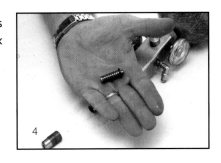

5

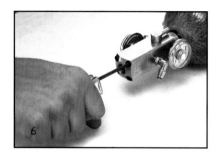

6. Take the piston housing off and inspect the regulator seat for any clues to problems you may have been experiencing. This is where we get into the regulator a little further than we would during regular maintenance. Troubleshooting a problem like broad swings in output flow, which may indicate a failed valve system, requires us to perform this inspection.

7. Inspect the white seating material (the little, white, plastic washer). Look for dirt, or the center hole appearing oblong instead of round, which would indicate that the pin is travelling in a direction that it shouldn't be. Then remove the regulator seating material from the piston housing with a pick.

8. Using a clean rag or preferably a cotton swab with a little bit of rubbing alcohol on it, clean all the mating surfaces of debris and oil. Pay close attention to the area that the regulator seat fits into.

The Complete Guide to Paintball

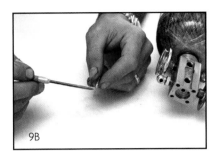

9B

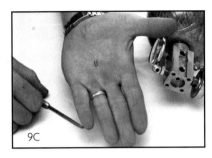

9C

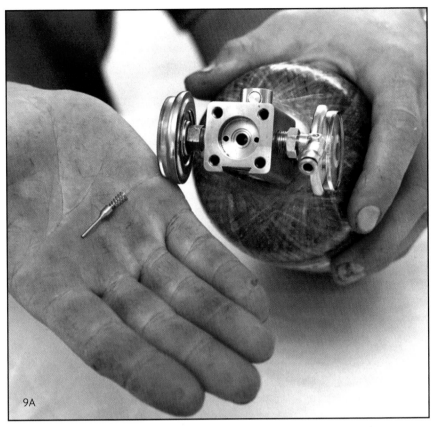

9A

9. Remove the regulating valve pin and the cone spring from the gas distribution body. Inspect them for any damage. Over-adjusting the regulator nut can bend the valve pin shaft. Make sure that the pin is straight and not marked up, and check that the cone spring isn't compressed or stretched due to improper installation. Watch for the natural compression that occurs with time and use.

10

10. Now, with a clean cotton swab or rag, clean the internal surfaces of the gas body, removing any debris, oil, or moisture.

11. This is as far as we go. After making sure that all of the surfaces are clean, we're going to work backwards and reassemble the regulator. The regulator seat (white washer) that we removed is made of hard urethane and can be used only once. It's a compression fitting. The two halves of the regulator, the gas distribution body and the piston housing, have sealing beads that make an indentation on the seat. Once you separate the two parts, the regulator seat needs to be replaced with a new one. Place the disk in the recessed area of the piston housing.

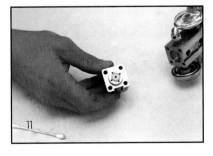

11

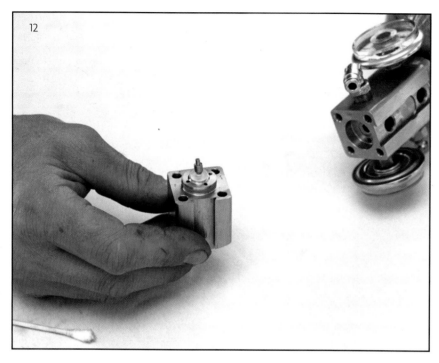

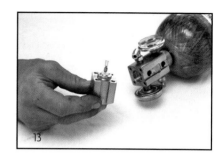

13. Replace the cone spring by fitting the tapered end on the short back-retaining shaft of the valve pin.

12. Now replace the valve pin by inserting the long shaft of the pin down through the regulator seat.

14. Firmly re-seat the piston housing on top of the gas distribution body. Fit the wider end of the cone spring into the recessed retaining pocket for the valve pin. Reinsert the four retaining screws. Take an Allen wrench and tighten the screws down gradually in a diagonal pattern. Tighten the opposite corners to evenly compress the seating material between the two halves. Tighten so that there's no gap between the piston housing and the gas distribution body, nice and snug, not over-torqued, but not just hand tight.

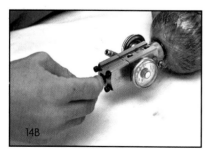

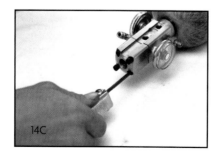

15A

15B

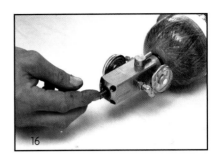

16

15. Lubricate the piston with a light coat of oil or silicone grease, and re-insert it flat-faced down, open end up, into the piston housing.

16. Insert a lightly lubricated mainspring into the piston.

17. Thread on the regular adjustment nut over the mainspring. At this point, we fill the bottle with nitrogen or compressed air, testing the regulator for any leaks.

Now you're ready to get back in the game!

17

18A

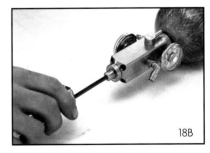

18B

18. Thread the tournament cap onto the regulator adjustment nut. Set your outgoing pressure using an Allen wrench, and lock down your tournament cap. Tighten its retaining screws.

LIKE A ROCK

Dennis Tippmann, Jr.

STEWART SMITH: Tippmann is the first name we heard of when we started out to make this book. How long have you been in the paintball business?

DENNIS TIPPMANN, JR: I've been doing this since 1986. So, it's been 13 years now. I don't know of any bigger companies in this industry that are older than we are.

STEW: As an established leader in the paintball industry, how do you explain your success?

DENNIS: We keep improving the quality and the price point of our products. The mass market volume sales we do enable us to do this, and our commitment to improving upon our guns in ways that are cost-effective for us and our customers keeps us ahead of the game.

STEW: Your guns are definitely affordable.

DENNIS: We make valuable guns that simply perform reliably and consistently over time. They're easy to maintain and we support our products very aggressively.

STEW: Your guns are also unique in that you diecast them in aluminum.

DENNIS: That's right. It definitely saves us money because we can avoid the more expensive class of machining.

STEW: Do you find the diecasting durable?

DENNIS: Oh, yes. Basically, it's the same material. Diecast aluminum is very tough.

STEW: How do you explain the popularity of your guns with field owners?

DENNIS: Rental places need our expertise. They need good, reliable, affordable guns, and they want the best CO_2 system guns they can buy. One thing we've always been good at is making great CO_2 guns. The rental guys need parts and service, too. That's another thing we do well. We get parts to them quickly. We offer one-year warranty on all our equipment. Because renters are more abusive and the gun gets used everyday, our support of fields is critical to their success.

They need a gun that's extremely durable, and a company to back it up. That's why they use our equipment.

STEW: Tell us about your Tippmann Model 98.

DENNIS: Sure. Our guns have always been solid, but we want to start introducing some of the high end advances to the mass market. Model 98 brings an advanced trigger system to the masses. Real high end guns go out of their way to build really good trigger systems, so that's where we've started. We've made the trigger really light on this gun, and it shoots very fast.

STEW: It's a reactive trigger?

DENNIS: Yeah, we call it the hyper-shot trigger. A light trigger with great response pressure. You see, on some guns with light triggers, the trigger doesn't swing back after you fire. We don't have that problem. The Model 98's return pressure gives you "lightness" speed and control.

STEW: So can you take the stock 98 out of the box, and add on bit by bit until you're up to a tournament level?

DENNIS: Yes. Absolutely. In fact, there are companies right now that are buying these receivers off us raw and doing stuff like this to them because we diecast that receiver. We don't have much money invested in the receiver anymore. So they're buying the receivers and making a number of little jazzy modifications to them. Double triggers and stuff like that.

As we're doing a lower-priced gun, we have the volumes real high. We can afford to diecast it. And then they can take that same diecasting, go and modify it, whatever they want.

STEW: Are you in any retail stores?

DENNIS: Wal-Marts and K-marts are what we're looking at right now. The guns are actually in Dicks, which is a sporting goods store, and some Sports Authority stores carry them.

STEW: What is an expansion chamber?

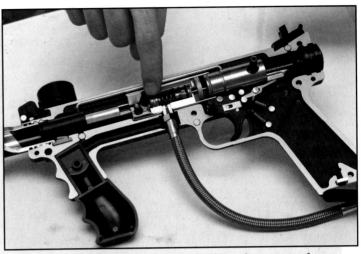

Dennis Tippmann, Jr. points out the CBX valve in this cutaway of a Model 98.

DENNIS: This is the first upgrade you would perform on a Tippmann Model 98. A lot of players put a barrel on right away and expansion chamber kit next.

Because CO_2 pressures go up and down, sometimes you'll get liquid CO_2 in your gun. Liquid CO_2 can be hard on a gun. You point your gun down, the liquid enters your gun and it responds by shooting really hard and erratic. The expansion chamber helps eliminate this effect. It makes it harder for liquid CO_2 to form and get into the valve of the gun. So it's just a way of making CO_2 work a little bit better.

STEW: Tell us about how your gun works.

DENNIS: When you pull the trigger on the gun, you release the bolt, and the rear bolt is connected to the front bolt. That'll shuttle a ball into the barrel. Now when the rear bolt gets clear forward, it hits the valve. When the valve is opened, pressure goes two directions. A very little bit goes to recock the gun, maybe 10%. The rest of it goes around the valve and shoots your ball. A little bit of pressure comes to the rear bolt, and recocks the gun. Normally, you wouldn't even be able to let off the trigger by the time the gun's recocked. The sear hits the back of the trigger, and then you let out the trigger and it reengages the top of the trigger for the next shot. There's a latch to hold the ball in place so it doesn't roll out your barrel until the trigger is pulled.

STEW: This latch is a piece of rubber?

DENNIS: Yeah. So, it's really a pretty simple system.

This is what they call a blow-back system. The bolt's blown back. There's two other systems. The blow-forward system, like your automatics, and the closed bolt system, which is like a pump gun with an automatic pump. What they mean by closed-bolt is that the bolt's forward, ready to fire. When you pull a trigger on a closed-bolt system, the bolt's closed. That means the bolt has already shut the chamber off. When you set the gun off, the ball's already in the barrel.

So the closed-bolt is like a pump gun, with an automatic pumper on it, like your Autocockers.

STEW: Autocockers are closed bolt?

DENNIS: Yeah. Automags are blow-forward, and mine are blow-back. Tippmann actually invented the blow-back system. We've got the patents on it.

STEW: The most efficient use of air would be the blow-back system?

DENNIS: They all run pretty neck and neck. I think the Model 98 is extremely efficient. But right now, I'd say probably the most efficient system besides this gun would be your closed-bolt system, which is found in Autocockers. They're extremely efficient because of the way they use the exact amount of air needed to cock the gun, and the exact amount of air needed to shoot the gun. Since the systems are all compartmentalized, it's easier for them to achieve high levels of efficiency. It took us a lot of tuning to get to that level. So Bud Orr's guns have been efficient for a long time.

And the next level we'd step up to is the CBX valve. It's our high performance valving system, and we're sure players will notice its advantages, particularly its reliability.

STEW: And this is something that you developed?

DENNIS: Yes. I do all the drawings. I make the prototypes. My father and I sit down and go over the designs before they're made. Some of the other guys actually cut some of the prototype parts. Some of our prototypes are cut out of solid aluminum. I'll draw a 3D model of the gun on my computer, which then actually talks to a milling machine. It writes a tool path that'll cut that shape out of a block of aluminum. So those prototypes are made out of solid aluminum. And that same software can be used to make a mold.

STEW: You have a family business. That's wonderful.

DENNIS: Yes, as far as design and conception. Yes, it really is.

STEW: Thank you for sharing your time and insights.

DENNIS: It was a pleasure.

Cleaning of a Tippmann Model 98

KEEP IT CLEAN

This is an ad hoc cleaning, the kind most recreational players will do after a solid day of play. Keep in mind that proper care and maintenance of your paintball gun will provide you with many years of reliable and safe fun. Of course, some people will leave their gear in a bag and worry about it tomorrow... but why should you?

You've made an investment in your gun and part of that investment is your time. Take the time to clean your gun after a day at the field.

I performed the following gun cleaning on a Tippmann Model 98 with a Lapco barrel.

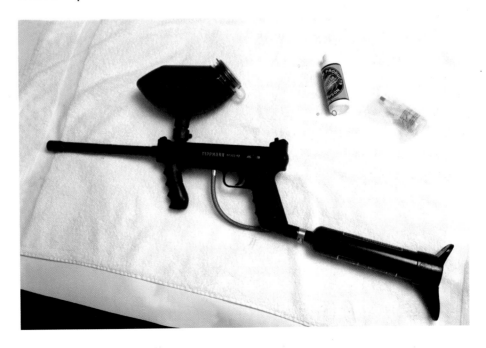

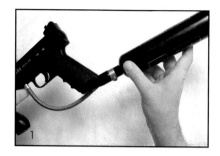

1. Remove the air tank first by turning slowly to release the pressure. Shoot the gun a few times to degas the entire air system. Note: shoot into a garbage can or cardboard box. Never into the air or at someone. And not with the barrel plug still in the gun.

2. Repeat this process, turning the air tank, and degassing the gun, until the bolt flops forward. This is an indication that it's okay to remove the air tank fully. The reason to take this care and not twist the air tank off fully in one go is to protect your o-rings.

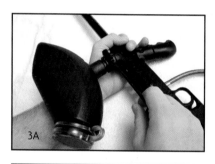

3. Using an Allen wrench, remove the loader from the feed neck by loosening the retaining bolt. Unique to the Tippmann feedneck is a set of "teeth" that grip the throat of the feeder. Don't try to yank the loader out. Loosen the retaining bolt (be careful not to lose the nut), and remove the loader when it pulls freely.

4. To clean the loader, stick your pinky in the feed neck, and check for paint. If it comes out dirty, wash the loader in the sink with some warm water.

PART 3

GEAR

To Thine Own Paintball Goals Be True

How to Make Sure You Have What You Need To Enjoy This Beautiful Game

The best way to choose your equipment is to analyze what kind of player you are, figure out where you're going to use the equipment, research the quality versus pricing issues, and then, *and only then*, spend your hard earned dollars accordingly.

Equipping yourself to play paintball is easy these days. Almost too easy. You basically have three choices: use what the advertisers say you should use, purchase the most expensive thing on the shelf, or get what your local dealer happens to have in stock today and "really likes." In reality, many players use one or another of these purchasing methods to equip themselves or their teams. That's sad, because it rarely leads to an optimal purchase.

Many people made "Home-brew" loaders from all sorts of objects. The most popular was an old oil can cleaned out, the top made into a lid, and placed onto the neck of a paintball gun. "D.A.M. cans" were a mass-produced version of the oil-can loaders. This design eventually lead to the mass-produced "Worr Games Ammo Box." This box held 45 paintballs, and had an opening for tubed paint (as in 10 round tubed paint). The WGP ammo box had the advantage of being smaller and more streamlined than the oil-can style of loaders. It was an instant hit.

Larger loaders were introduced very quickly. The first was the "Whaler," which resembled a large sausage tube with "Magic Fish Lips" (no, I'm not making this up!) to aid in faster loading. The need for a better loader was answered by Viewloader, a company that introduced a modular 90-round hopper simply called "Viewloader." It had a clear flip lid, which was easy to look into and to load on the fly.

Viewloader also made 45-round hoppers with which one could fill this new loader. Other companies used this same principle to create a plethora of 100–150 capacity loaders. This was the norm, with a few larger loaders becoming available.

The only problem with all this was the paint. Many paintball guns wouldn't create enough of a 'kick' to move the paint around, and jams were common. Imagine having to shoot five times, shake your gun, shoot another 5 times, shake your gun, and doing this all day. Players wanted a solution, and Viewloader delivered one.

Viewloader created the first patented agitating loader, the VL-2000. It works by placing an electronic eye in the feed neck that tells a motherboard to rotate a paddle to move the paintballs around in the loader. They originally designed it on their 200 round loader, but with time and research it's become streamlined and efficient. Many players agree that the 200 round loader is the best for size, weight, and capacity.

The latest in high-technology is based on the VL-2000, called the "VL-2001." It's an electronic loader that you plug into the gun itself. The motor rotates and agitates the balls at a predetermined trigger pull. Electropneumatic paintguns like the Angel or the Shocker use this kind of loader, as the guns themselves are electronics-based.

Other loaders are still available. For example Indian Springs makes a 125 paintball hopper that's well suited for pump guns, if you're into vintage old-school play. Many other companies and loaders exist as well. Keep your eyes open for the next best thing—force-feed. But for the time being you have many excellent loaders to choose from.

-RR

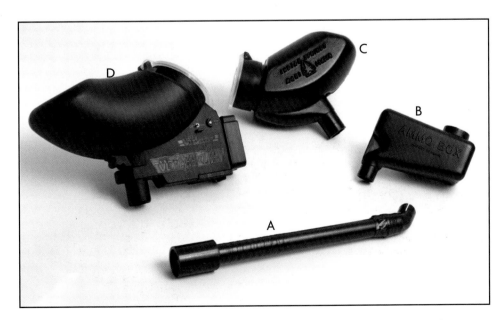

Brief History of the Loader

A. 15 round stick feeder

B. Worr Games Product Ammo Box

C. Indian Springs 120 round loader

D. View Loader Revolution, Brass Eagle, with VL timer

Squeegees in a Nutshell

The Fine Art of Squeegee

WHERE TO START

There are two basic styles of squeegees on the market. Picking one is a matter of objective necessity and personal preference. Both clean out your barrel very effectively, but you may like one more than the other.

The first style is a "Stick" squeegee. "Stick" squeegees are long plastic tubes with a rubber disc at one end, and a spring-style action at the other end. To use this effectively, you push down on one end to push the rubber disk out. You need to flatten the disk out, and push it down the barrel.

When you release the top spring, the disk comes flat against the plastic tube, filling the barrel. When you pull out the squeegee, it pulls broken paint and shell out with it. Many styles have a cloth on the opposite end, with which you can clean any residual paint out of your barrel.

The other style is a "Pull Through" or "Cable" squeegee. The cable style has several disks on a cord, and sometimes a fluffy "Swab" on the end. To use one, you need to remove the barrel from the paintball gun. You place the end without the disks in one end of the barrel, feeding it to the other side. You then pull on that end to bring the disks through the barrel, cleaning out the paint in your barrel. The "Swab" removes anything that may be left in the barrel, making one clean sweep.

Both styles have advantages and disadvantages.

- Stick squeegees are easy to use and you'll be done in a jiffy, but they may not clean the barrel as effectively as a pull through.

- A pull through can't be used on some styles of paintball guns with "Fixed" (non-removable) barrels.

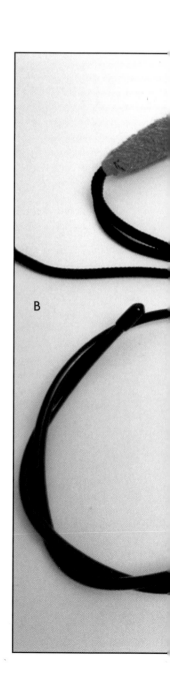

B

- The phase of the moon. (Just kidding, but you get the point. Many things affect your paintball's path!)

Adco Hot Shot, Adco vision 2000

Smart Parts HI VIZ

Where a paintball is going to go is often an unknown. So, the scope usually out-performs the paint. This isn't to say that a scope or sight is useless. I've had a lot of success using them on my personal paintguns. You just need to understand a few guidelines for the use of these accessories so that you can optimize your experience of them.

HOW TO USE SIGHTS & SCOPES TO IMPROVE YOUR GAME

My opinion is that scopes have limited usefulness. Why? Magnification interferes with your aim. Your magnified perspective will usually be further ahead than the ball will travel. That said, I grant that sights and scopes are useful for looking downfield in the larger "big game" formats of paintball. In other words, use the magnification to look a couple hundred yards ahead to see if your competition is moving around out there, where they're headed, things like this. Of course, opportunities to do this are few and far between for most people. In most cases, you want a sight with no magnification that simply puts a "dot" in space.

Once you've gotten your sight, you want to "Dial it in." What is *dialing*? In an ideal scenario, realize that a sight can only tell you where the barrel is pointed, not where your paint will eventually go. A little experimentation will tell you where paint is likely to go when you're aiming at something within a certain range. If you can hit a pie-plate at 75 feet, you can calibrate or 'dial' your sight so that it will reflect where the paint usually goes at that dis-

tance. This takes some time and patience. I like to dial in at 75–100 feet, as most of my shooting happens within that range.

In regular "toe-to-toe" play, you usually don't use sights. I find myself just shooting and following where the last ball went, or using the barrel itself as a large point sight. For long angle shots, or for ambush situations, sights work very well. My personal technique may not work for everyone, but it's worth trying.

Place the dot on your opponent's chest area. If a ball drifts in most any direction, it will still probably hit them. I like to keep both eyes open for a stereoscopic view, but some prefer to close one eye to concentrate on the shot. Either way works well. Then, simply pull the trigger in the same way that you would any other time. Don't change that detail, because if you do it won't "feel" right and you probably won't hit the person. Paintguns have no recoil, so slow trigger pulls aren't necessary. In some cases, it may not give you the best shot. Some players put a short "string" of 3 balls on a target, but sometimes that's not necessary.

Using a sight or a scope may or may not improve your game. Your best bet is to invest in an inexpensive sight to try it out. If it helps your game or you just really enjoy using it, you'll find no shortage of variety in terms of available scopes and sights.

—RR

Armson/Pro-Team Products
Pro-Drop Red Dot

PART 4

DRILLS

Warm Up
Play Hot

Prepare Your Body to Optimize Your Game Play

After interviewing some of the top paintball players and paintball field owners in the world, it was apparent that many of the injuries that occur during a paintball game could be easily avoided by a moderate level of fitness and flexibility. In fact, the two biggest injuries are ankle sprains and muscle pulls (hamstrings and lower back). The ankle injuries can be decreased by wearing proper shoes such as high top cleats and a few basic calf exercises and stretches. The hamstrings and the lower back can also be strengthened by a easy routine of stretching and exercising. This chapter is devoted not only to preventing the most common injuries in paintball, but to assisting adventurous paintball players in becoming more flexible, faster, stronger, and healthier. Follow this step-by-step stretching program during the week and you will be able to splat your opponents with ease during the weekend paintball games.

Stewart Smith graduated from the United States Naval Academy in 1991. He then spent four years on SEAL teams, after which he was put in charge of the physical training and selection of future BUD/S candidates. Stewart currently runs the getfitnow.com family fitness center in Severna Park, Maryland.

WARMING-UP

Warming up prior to stretching, exercise, and playing paintball is absolutely crucial to injury prevention. You will find that your muscles are more flexible and react to stretching far better after a brief 5–10 minute warm-up. Do this by walking, jogging slowly, riding a bike, or doing 50 jumping jacks.

The objective is to get your heart pumping above its normal rate, which will increase the blood flow to the muscles that you are about to stretch and use. Stretching is not only the best way to avoid injuries, but also the best way to prepare yourself to get tight and small behind a bunker, and then explode in a sprint on the attack. Regardless of your age, paintball is a vigorous and challenging sport that will test your stamina. To take your game to the next level, give your body the attention it needs, and follow these simple guidelines.

YO!

We'll be covering only stretches in this book, so we encourage you to check out our workout resources for the active sports enthusiast by visiting the GetFitNow.com web site. As most of our workout books are derived from the finest fitness regimens in the world, those of our United States Armed Forces, we are certain that you will find them extremely helpful in training to become the ultimate paintball warrior!

S T R E T C H E S

UPPER AND LOWER BODY

Arm (Shoulder)

Drop your shoulder and pull your arm across your chest. With the opposite arm, gently pull your arm across your chest and hold for 15 seconds. Repeat with the other arm.

This stretches the back of the shoulder and muscles that attach the shoulder blade to the upper part of the back. This is the very root of most tension headaches. Keeping these muscles flexible will help prevent injuries caused by running and falling to the ground when you are seeking cover from incoming paintballs.

The Most Advanced Piece of Machinery in Paintball? Your Body.

Arm Circles

Rotate your arms slowly in big circles forward and then reverse. This will help prepare your shoulders for pushups, dips, and dumbbell work.

Triceps into Lateral Stretch

Place both arms over and behind your head. Grab your right elbow with your left hand and pull your elbow toward your opposite shoulder. Lean with the pull. Repeat with the other arm.

This stretch prepares you for the dumbbell triceps exercises, pushups, and dips, but also helps stretch the back muscles. This is a very important stretch for upper body exercises!

Chest

Stand with your arms extended and parallel to the floor. Slowly pull your elbows back as far as you can. Hold for 15 seconds. Do not thrust your arms backwards. This is a slow and deliberate stretch designed to prepare your chest for pushups, dips, and other shoulder/chest exercises.

Shoulder Rotations

Rotate your shoulders slowly up and down, keeping your arms relaxed by your side. Your shoulders should rotate in small circles and move up and down in slow distinct movements.

Stomach Stretch

Lie on your stomach. Push yourself up to your elbows. Slowly lift your head and shoulders and look up at the sky or ceiling. Hold for 15 seconds and repeat two times.

Hip Rotations

Place your hands on your hips and slowly rotate your hips in big circles clockwise and counter-clockwise for about 15 seconds in each direction.

In a game where a miss is as good as a mile, an extra show of agility, degree of flexibility, or burst of speed can make the difference between Triumph and Defeat!

Thigh Stretch On Ground

Lie on your left side. Pull your right foot to your butt by grabbing your ankle and hold it with your right hand. Keep your knees close together and hold for 10–15 seconds. Repeat with the other leg.

Calf Stretch / Achilles Tendon Stretch

Stand with one foot 2–3 feet in front of the other. With both feet pointing in the same direction you are facing, put most of your body weight on the leg that is behind you, stretching the calf muscle.

Now, bend the rear knee slightly. You should now feel the stretch in your heel. This stretch helps prevent achilles tendonitis, a severe injury that will sideline most paintball players for at least 4–6 weeks.

Hamstring Stretch

From the standing or sitting position, bend forward at the waist and touch your toes. Keep your back straight and slightly bend your knees. You should feel this stretching the back of your thighs near the connection of the leg and butt. Now, slowly straighten your legs, feeling the stretch travel down your leg and behind your knees. You have just stretched the entire hamstring. Hold both the straight leg and bent leg stretch for 15 seconds each.

Most people pull their hamstring at the top part of the leg (where it connects to the buttocks). By simply bending your knees while stretching, you will decrease your chances of suffering the most common injury to paintball players.

Groin/Inner Thigh Side Stretch

Stand with your legs spread and lean to the left. Keep the right leg straight while pointing the toes up. Repeat on the other side. This will help prevent groin strains, another common injury to paintball players who play speedball and games with a similar fast-paced tempo.

Hurdler Stretch

Sit on the floor with your legs straight in front of you. Bend your right knee and place the bottom of your foot on the inside of your opposite thigh. With your back straight, lean forward in order to stretch the back of your legs and lower back. Hold the stretch for 15 seconds, switch legs, and repeat.

Ilio Tibial Stretch

Sit on the ground with your legs crossed in front of you. Keeping your legs crossed, bring the top leg to your chest and bend it at the knee so that your foot is placed outside of your thigh. Hold for 15 seconds and repeat with the other leg.

You should perform this stretch before and after running. This will help prevent very common over-use injuries in the hips and knees.

Knees-to-Chest

Lie flat on your back. Pull your knees to your stomach and hold for 20 seconds. You should perform this stretch before and after any abdominal exercise.

As you may know, the lower back is the most commonly injured area of the body. Many lower back problems stem from inactivity, lack of flexibility, and improper lifting of heavy objects. Stretching and exercising your lower back will help prevent injuries to this extremely sensitive area.

Butterfly

Sit on your buttocks with your knees bent and the soles of your feet together. Grab your ankles and place both of your elbows on your inner thighs. Slowly push down on your thighs.

AND NOW YOU'RE READY TO RUMBLE

Underestimating the stress you put on your body when playing this game is a surefire way to get injured or develop chronic aches and pains. If you do these stretches every day, and always perform them before playing paintball, you will be doing yourself a huge favor.

Stewart Smith's Paintball Workout is available on our web site, GetFitNow.com, for those of you interested in the achieving the highest possible performance.

PAUL FOGAL ON FITNESS
Fitness Does Matter

"I think one of the beauties of paintball is that just about anybody can play because you can play to your level of fitness. If you're scared or you're slow or you have a disability or something, you can play a static defense. You can guard the flag. You can be a central source of communication. You have options people who aren't in the best shape don't have in other sports. And if you happen to be in great shape and you're real aggressive, then you can go out on offense and you can run.

It certainly helps to be in some kind of shape, because then you really have your choice of how you want to play. And, of course, small, quick people definitely have an advantage. It's harder to hit a quick and small target. You don't have to be in particularly great shape to enjoy paintball, but the better shape you're in, the more options you have."

Stretch out and you'll feel better before, during, and after you play!

Tactical Drills
for the
Beginner

TO KICK ASS, YOU MUST DRILL!

Our goal in this chapter is to teach paintball playing basics.
Of course, you can tailor paintball tactics drills as you see fit.
The key is not merely to practice, but to practice the right
things.

FIRST THINGS FIRST

Chronograph your paintgun to 285–290 feet per second (fps), the appropriate outdoor playing speed.

Each drill is a scenario. The object of each scenario is similar to what you will face on a normal playing day in both recreational and tournament play. Once you know the moves, you can repeat them with minimal effort. Think of them as "katas" of sorts.

Each drill should be performed from "both ends" if applicable. The idea is to combine all of the aspects of the game into your individual game. Even in a team setting, your individual moving, shooting, and communication skills will make or break a game.

SHOOTING DRILLS

You'll need the following supplies: Paper Plates (pie tins, frisbees, etc.), a stopwatch.

Obstacle course

Object—Run the course as fast as you can, hitting all the targets as you do so. This is a sample course, feel free to adjust it to your conditions and playing field. Just remember that the course should resemble a playing field as accurately as possible.

- On breakout, hit a 100 foot target

- From a bunker position, hit 75' and a 50' targets

- Run to new bunker, shoot a 75' offhanded shot (lefty for right-handers, righty for left-handers)

- Run to new position, shooting at a positioned plate as you pass it. (This is called bunkering or a 'takedown').

- From new bunker, take offhand 50', 75' shots, then regular hand 75', 50' shots.

The Complete Guide to Paintball

- Take a 150' long shot from new position, then turn around for a 25' close shot.

- Stop watch at flag station bunker. Repeat the course until you improve your time and accuracy. Then change the course to give yourself a fresh challenge.

A SIMPLE RUN & SHOOT DRILL

Another simple Run & Shoot Drill is to set up a series of targets (in this case soda jugs hanging from a rope) and run past them, shooting as you go. Your motion, as well as the swinging of the jugs makes this a particularly challenging drill.

Of course, you do have options...

Two player option: Follow the same course with a player shooting at you as you run through it.

Team option: On the same course, one player moves while the second gives cover fire. When the target is hit, the second player leapfrogs to the next position.

Pressure option: Same course, teammate runs course behind you. If you do not hit your target before your teammate does, your teammate is allowed to shoot you to get you to move.

BACKFOOT TACTICS DRILL

Timed Offense/Defense

Needed—At least 2 players, position of defense (such as a flag station or a building), flag, stopwatch.

Setup—3 attackers to 2 defenders *or* 2 attackers to 1 defender

Scenario—For each defender, put 1 minute and 30 seconds on the clock.

Goals

- Defense must prevent a flag pull.
- Offense must grab the flag and get away clean in the time allotted.
- Offense may set up anywhere beyond 150 feet of the defensive flag.
- Defense may set up anywhere within 150 feet of the flag, the closer the better.

Lessons

Offense—Must be aggressive when the numbers are in their favor, and learn to push hard under time pressure.

Defense—Learn how to be patient and kill a clock when outnumbered. Survival is the key, and staying in the game under pressure is hard.

This drill can also be used to simulate defending an opponents' flag station while they are trying to bring your flag in for a win. For this, do 3 on 1. Your solo guy gets a minute to set up. The aggressors have 2 minutes to hang the flag.

WORKING WITH BUNKERS

All bunkers "work" (or *are worked*) in the same manner. Flat-sided ones are easier to demonstrate on. The drills I'm highlighting here apply for use of trees, brambles, or any similar protection.

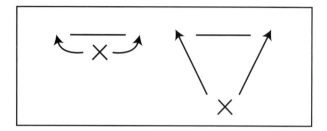

Take A Few Steps Back To Gain Perspective and Expand Your Field of Vision and Kill Zone

Get back if you can. You can cover more space with less effort.

Be Unpredictable

Move around in a position, because "Jack in the Boxes" get hit.

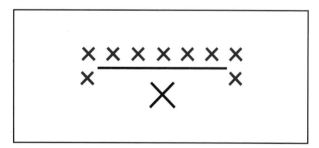

The little red markers represent all of the potential angles from which "X" can pop up and take shots at his opponents. Being unpredictable keeps your opponents waiting for your next move.

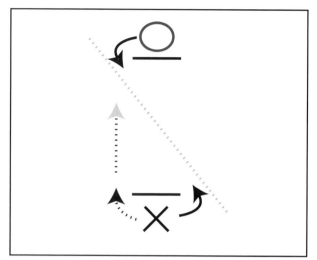

When "X" sees that "O" keeps emerging from the left side, he suspects his opponent is right-handed and relies too much on firing from the same place. They exchange fire along the pink line several times. Then, by shifting to the left side of his bunker and using his left hand, "X" surprises "O", and gets the elimination. "X" is right-handed, but he practices left-handed shooting to gain the advantage in scenarios like this one.

Downfall of the "Right Hand" Conspiracy

Actually, what we're talking about here has absolutely nothing to do with a conspiracy. It just happens to be the case that most people are right-handed and have a natural propensity to favor the right side of their bunker. From your perspective, that means most opponents will be emerging from the left side of their bunker. If you practice shooting with your off hand, you can make better use of your cover to eliminate your opponent.

This is pretty powerful knowledge, but you need to practice taking advantage of it!

Go the other way and take opponents out before they know what hit them.

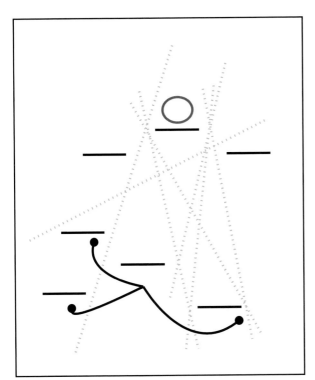

By moving behind different bunkers, even moving backwards, "X" is able to attain new angles of attack against "O." The dotted lines are shooting lanes that "X" can take advantage of if he's willing to take new positions.

Be Dynamic—Move From Bunker to Bunker To Gain New Angles of Attack

Use all the space you have available, even if it means falling back or shifting sideways. One person can take up a lot of space.

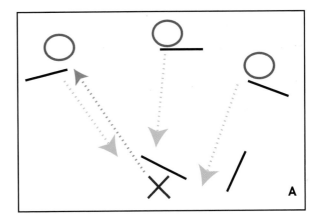

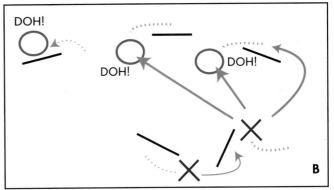

(A) "X" is in a tough spot. One moment, he's occupying two opponents. The next, he finds himself wide open to a flanking "O." While calling for support from teammates, "X" must act fast to maintain his position, using fire to literally "cover" his own position. This can't last for long!

(B) With support from a stealthy teammate who heard his coded plea for assistance, "X" is able to turn the opponents' perception of his weakness against them. As they move in for the kill, they are taken out by "X"'s flanking teammate. Now it's 2-on-1 in favor of our resourceful team "X" who quickly take new positions. *Never give up!*

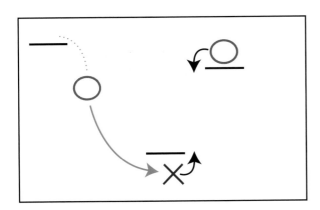

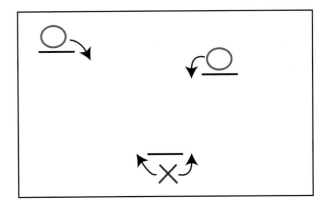

"X" is focused on the "O" right in front of him. This is exactly what Team "O" is counting on. A preoccupied "X" is easy to flank, as we can see from the first diagram. "X" is about to become "American History X."

A more mature "X" is moving in his bunker and looking for enemies on all sides. Here he has a good chance of keeping two opponents at bay, even taking them both out. Observe that if "X" has practiced using both left and right hands, he'll be more effective at keeping his opponents on their heels. Never stop moving behind your bunker. "X" should also communicate that he has two "O"'s in from of him and try to turn the tables on them with help from teammates! "X" may also want to try 'taking a few steps back' to facilitate handling this relatively precarious situation.

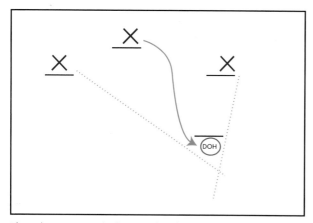

The Ultimate DOH! This is what happens to someone who doesn't communicate and doesn't play as part of a team. Or someone on a team that has been demolished!

If you're the only one left, and you find yourself completely overwhelmed, you still have options. As you can see, if "O" doesn't move, he's a goner. May as well try to take out as many of the opposition as he can!

**Avoid tunnel vision!
In a bunker, keep looking and shooting both ways to keep your enemies at bay.**

Look for natural holes in cover (like barrels) and shoot through them.

HERO TIME!

DELUSIONS OF INVINCIBILITY CAN BE USEFUL

Sometimes you need to act in a manner that others will perceive as incredibly daring and maybe even a little crazy. But in reality, a grand (or gutsy) move can blow open a game. Your opponents may fall into the trap of expecting you to be as cautious as they are. Suddenly, you're heading for an extremely aggressive position. They may get distracted by your audacity and pause before responding. If you pull it off, they'll feel demoralized and may be inclined to become preoccupied with your ominous position.

"I can't believe that guy just did that. What's he going to do next?"

These are just a few of the questions that you can implant in the minds of your foe with a bold move!

Another benefit of this is that it takes the heat off of your teammates, who should be able to take better positions while the other team is second-guessing itself. Of course, you should scream at your team to do this if they're not responding promptly.

Aggression can be rewarded, as long as you are in control and know what is going on.

DRILLING FOR DOUBLES

Coordinating your game play with one other person makes you a double-threat both defensively and offensively. The following drills will enable you to practice basic coordination techniques that can lead to dramatic results in games. You'll take a couple of steps closer to an elevated understanding of paintball when you practice working in teams. Drilling 2-on-2 is a great way to work on coordinated offense and defense.

Low Man Approach With Cover
High man supplies cover by shooting over crawler. Crawler takes new position and shoots opponent.

Flank'em
One flanks left while other teammate shoots to keep opponent occupied and down. Flanker shoots opponent from new position.

Overbound
One moves, the other takes his place. This is called displacing. Keep moving up like the ends of a centipede.

DRILLING FOR VICTORY

SNAP SHOOTING DRILL

If you have been placed into your bunker and cannot come out, snap shooting allows you to take one or two shots to get your opponent back into his bunker, giving you an opportunity to get out. It is important not to come out from the same spot twice in a row. You change the spots you come out from so opponents won't know where to expect you.

When practicing snap shooting drills, make sure you have someone there to point out areas you are leaving exposed (e.g., your hopper or elbows and knees).

GOOD FORM IS CRITICAL

Left, right, center, it doesn't matter where you come from as long as you never repeat the same pattern twice.

RUNNING MAN DRILL

The purpose of this drill is to learn how to shoot into the empty space that a target is going to enter just in time to hit it. This is called *leading*.

Use a live moving target—with that person's consent, of course—and stage it so he or she is running perpendicular to your position. Lead the person by putting a stream of paint into the direction they are moving, or over the bunker they are heading toward.

It is good to start at a distance of 100–150 feet. Shoot about 10–15 feet in front of your target, and have that daring soul run his or her fastest. There's no time factor in this exercise, but try to limit the number of rounds to about 20 per drill before starting over.

Drilled Running Man

The Complete Guide to Paintball

By increasing the angle of your barrel, you will be able to increase the distance your paintballs will fly. At some point, of course, you shorten the distance the paintball will travel, but increase the slope of its descent.

LONG DISTANCE SHOOTING DRILL

When practicing long distance shooting drills, set up a target 200–210 feet in front of you. Limit the number of rounds in the hopper to time the drill and the number of shots you take. This drill teaches players how to control the arc of their ball so they can get the maximum range out of their shooting skill. Being a long distance shooter with accuracy is a fast track to legendary status in paintball lore.

At 200 feet, paintballs don't break that easily, as Steve points out. The longer the ball is in the air, the less energy it will have on impact.

Hopper Loading Drill

Learn to load your hopper without taking your eyes off the action. At first, perform this drill with an empty hopper and empty guppies. Get the motion down first before using paint (to avoid getting it dirty). With one hand holding your gun, perform your loading routine as follows:

A. Pop your loader's lid open.

B. Reach behind you and open your velcro harness.

C. Firmly grab a full guppy and bring it forward.

D. Pop the guppy's lid with your thumb.

E. Dump paint into your loader.

F. With the bottom of the now empty guppy, flip the loader's lid closed and snap the lid tight.

G. Toss the guppy aside and resume firing.

NOTE: This should be one smooth continuous motion. Practice until you get it right! Practice while you watch your favorite television shows and time yourself.

Blind Shooting Drill

There are times in a game where you are shooting without a clear view of your target. In these cases, you are "shooting blind." Blind shooting can be an effective shooting technique. The key is learning to identify a reference point that you can see from your firing position that relates directly to your opponent's position. This way you can stay safe in your bunker while you rain paint down on your opponent's head. He'll get dumped with paint and you can move on to your next unwitting target.

To practice, you and your buddy face off in opposite bunkers. From a quick peek, see if there is an object directly in line with their position. In this sequence you'll notice a tree directly behind your opponent's position in the background. Now, from the safe haven of your bunker, lay a stream of paint in the direction of the tree without overexposing yourself to return fire. Change the angle of your barrel to increase or decrease the range of your fire. By getting used to the feel of blind shooting in this manner, you'll increase your chances of survival, and become more of an offensive threat.

Out of paint?
Keep shooting anyway. The sound will keep your opponents' heads down while your teammates gain advantageous positions.

Out of air?
Throw paintballs. Heck, it'll keep them guessing and one just might break!

PART 5

TACTICS

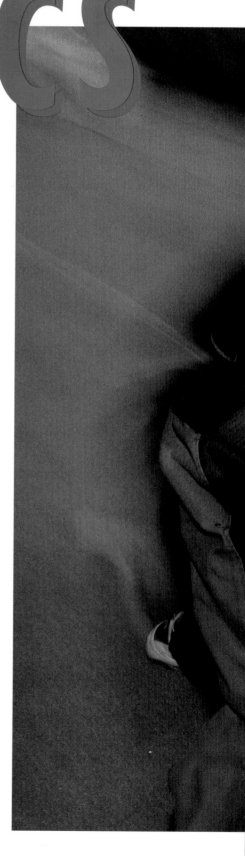

A.C.T.

Rob Rubin's Customized Approach to Essential Paintball Tactics

"GETTING" PAINTBALL

When you first start playing paintball, you're literally bombarded with suggestions, advice, and ideas about the game. As is the case with most new players in any sport, it's easy to get overwhelmed just trying to keep up.

There's an easy way around "Information Overload."

You see, I've done a little work to fix this problem. And the good news for you is that paintball can be boiled down to a simple formula that's not only easy to remember, but even easier to carry out.

I call this "The Triad." It will carry you very far in your pursuit of paintball fun. You see, the game is only fun up to the point of elimination. Learning tactics is about learning how to stay in the game.

And the core of paintball tactics is the Triad.

Here it is.

A.C.T.-UNG Baby!

"Angles" "Communications" "Teamwork"

These are the three basics of paintball, "A.C.T." for short. That's all you need to know. This may sound simplistic, but even professional teams are always working on these three basic principles. Forget the gizmos, forget the gadgets, forget the tech-talk. These are the nuts and bolts of the game. If you want to be somewhere between competent and excellent at paintball, you must master "the Triad."

Why "The Triad"?

Much like a tripod, this particular trio of paintball skills works only as a whole. When you play them all, you get a whole game. It's easier to explain how they interconnect by looking at them in reverse order.

Do It For the Team

Teamwork can be as complex as 10 players moving as one mind, or as simple as finding a buddy and moving together up the tapeline. A second pair of eyes is invaluable, and a second shooter on a target can be the difference between wasting your time and eliminating your opponent.

Teamwork doesn't mean you're on top of one another, but it does mean you're working together for a common goal. One player is shooting at the opponent, the other player is advancing on him. That's great teamwork. One player is yelling positions, the other players are listening and moving accordingly. That's effective teamwork.

You can even have teamwork when you don't know anyone you're playing with!

In open fields or speedball games, I'll be the fool yelling his head off about where I saw players running to, or where they have people positioned. Why? Someone has to, and it may as well be me. Something as simple as "3 right, 4 left, 2 center" tells your team how they stack up against their foes. *Communication accomplishes teamwork.*

Communication = Effective Yelling

Sure, anyone can yell their lungs out. But it's effective yelling that makes the difference. Remember that teamwork thing? Here's the second part of it—communication.

Once you've buddied up, or you've decided to be a 'caller,' don't be shy. If you need some help, a simple "Help here!" gets the message across. You can get someone to move up to help you, or flank around to eliminate the opposing player who's shooting at you, and a lot of other things too.

New players often try to be 'stealthy,' and that works up to a point. One of my rules of thumb: "Once the other team shoots at you, don't bother trying to hide anymore." They've spotted you. It's useless to hide now. What you want to do immediately is get another player to help you out. Give them as much information as you can. For example:

"There are two guys in that bunker! Can you swing around and shoot them?" This brings us to the third leg—angles.

Angles

The term 'angles' covers moving, maneuvering, crawling, leaping, getting skinny behind a tree, and getting into a bunker so the other team can't occupy it.

Paintball is partially a game of real-estate, and getting angles is the way you use real-estate effectively. As an individual player, you want to take advantage of opponents who get 'tunnel vision' (players fixated on what's in front of them) by moving up on their flanks. A tree can only protect from so many directions at a given moment. The key is getting to an angle that renders your opponent's tree useless.

Your most frequent use of angles is to support your teammates. Most shoot-outs take place head on, meaning face to face. The idea behind 'angles' is to get to the side of your opponent while your teammate keeps your opponent's attention. After you make that key elimination, your teammate begins to move up while you support his advance similarly.

Pretty cool, isn't this?

You may already be starting to see the pattern. You can't "do" one part of the Triad well without doing the other two simultaneously.

- If you don't communicate, your teammates won't know you need them to take a better angle on the player shooting at you.

- If your team won't move to better angles, your teamwork breaks down and you get eliminated quickly.

- If you don't work together at all, you'll find the day frustrating, because your team won't communicate and move together in any way.

A.C.T. is a simple formula, and it encompasses the essence of what you need to do to qualify as a great player. It's also adaptable to your later paintball games as well. The concept of "Angles" includes 'back doors' and 'key bunkers' and seeing holes in your opponent's line. Simple "communications" later become your team codes. And "Teamwork" becomes the backbone of your game.

Putting It All Together

Eventually you combine the elements of the Triad into complex "Swing" moves and "Sweep" maneuvers.

For example, the "Two Man Swing" uses all of "A.C.T." in rapid order. Your buddy starts by telling you the opponent's position (communication), you start shooting to keep your opponent's head down (teamwork) as your buddy moves up (angles), you continue to feed your buddy information about where the opponent is (communications/teamwork) as he slides into his new position (angles). Your buddy begins to shoot (teamwork) and tell you where the opponent is leaning out of (communications) as you move up (angles) to get the elimination.

All of this may occur within ten seconds.

For now, don't worry about achieving that level of play. It takes practice, a good memory, and adventurous spirit to get good at this game. All of that takes time.

For now, have a good time! Enjoy yourself! Try to remember to "A.C.T." Write it on the back of your hand if need be. Talk to your teammates about it, too. It's something that everyone and anyone can do with a little effort.

—RR

Once you have the Triad down, you'll be amazed how fast it can improve your game.

of eliminating the opposition and winning the game.

So you can see that by getting your team to concentrate on technical aspects of play, everything else seems to fall into place. Even if you're not on a team, it should be clear to you that honing your technique will enable you to survive longer when you're on a losing team, and may make victory possible when you're outnumbered.

A LOOK AT THE ACTUAL TECHNIQUES!

Now that we have established the importance of technical play, we have to look at what those techniques are, in terms of what to do and what not to do.

First off, we can reduce the game of paintball, in simple terms to ten one-on-ones. For the moment, I am using a ten man tournament team as an example, although what is to be discussed is wholly applicable to players at all levels.

If a target player is beading on me (i.e., lining his gun up on me and occasionally firing when I come out to fire at him), then there are a couple of things to remember.

First of all, never come out into an incoming stream of paint. Seems obvious, but you would be surprised just how many mugs do it. You have to wait until your opponent stops firing at you. Alternatively, you can move to the other side of the bunker, but this normally means you will be shooting back-handed, so I will ignore that option for the moment.

If you are right-handed, I take it for granted that you are shooting out of the right hand side of the bunker as you look at it. The reason is obvious; you show a minimum profile to your opponents if you shoot this way. That brings us to snap shooting.

Snap Shooting 101

Accepting that we never break cover into a stream of paint, we now have to create an opportunity to fire at our target. When your opponent stops firing, the best technique is to snap shoot your way into dominance. If your opponent is lined up and just waiting for you to come out, then this is what you should do.

Get in to your mind the approximate location of your opponent. You can do this quite easily by taking a quick look in the direction from which the sound of your opponent's gun is coming. You should already have a good sense of his location because you know he's generally going to be sitting behind a bunker just like yours.

Once you have established his location, then get yourself set to roll out of cover with an upper-body roll movement.

This takes a bit of practice, but generally I would sit with my legs in front of me, usually bent in front of my chest, in a position behind the bunker that just allows me to be safe. In other words, if I were to lean slightly outwards to the right, my opponent could eliminate me, but with a slight roll back in, he would not be able to see me, let alone tag me.

When you're set, roll out, fire two shots, and immediately roll back in. The reason for this rapid-movement, minimal-fire approach is simple. If your opponent has indeed lined up where you're likely to emerge, you have to take a shot at him and get behind cover before you get hit. That's not long at all; if you only shoot twice and roll back in, there is no way that your opponent can react in time to eliminate you. The window of opportunity you gave him is just too small, he will always be one step off the pace you are setting.

If you adhere to this technique, the only way you can get tagged is if your opponent fires randomly and gets lucky.

If you roll out of cover, and a paintball is already winging it's way over to you, you're a goner!

So there remain now two possibilities in this interaction.

1. You eliminate him by snap shooting
2. You have to modify your technique slightly

As you roll in and out of cover and fire your two-shot bursts, you are relying on a fair amount of luck to get your elimination. Nevertheless, many players are eliminated this way.

The reason you have to roll in and out of cover is because your opponent has the drop on you.

The key here is to turn the tables and get the drop on him!

At present, it looks as though he controls things by making you snap shoot, but what if we could push him back into cover leaving us to line up on him?

To put your opponent on the defensive, you must do two things when you come out to snap shoot. First, watch as you roll back into cover; you are looking for any movement of your opponent that suggests your two shots are so accurate that they forced him to get back behind his bunker. Secondly, listen carefully, because if you hear no shots coming back at you right away, it's likely that you forced him back, but failed to see it.

If you are looking for them, these two clues give you a chance to establish control of the situation. If you take advantage of them, you can line up on the guy who thought he had you right where he wanted you!

Suppress your opponent with protracted fire enabling one of your teammates to bunker him. At the very least, keep him out of the game with continuous shooting.

The big advantage in lining up an opponent is that you get a chance to 'read' all of his movements. After observing him for a while, you'll find that he becomes predictable. This predictability will eventually be his downfall. Be patient and persistent, and you'll know this fine feeling.

In everything having to do with paintball technique, the key is concentration. You must concentrate on staying tight to your cover and on timing your retaliatory fire.

This is the way to optimize your chances of eliminating your opponent and minimize your chances of getting shot.

We have now covered two of the most fundamental aspects of paintball technique. Whether you are an experienced pro or a first timer, staying tight and timing your shots will transform your game overnight.

-PR

Mapping Your Game Plan

The Fake and Push

The fake and the push can be used on any field, but must be adjusted according to terrain. A critical component of this and any game plan is that your team should walk onto the field together. Each player must examine his own bunker and firing lanes. Both sides of the field must be walked. It is important to know what positions the opposing team may take. This will help you calculate the firing lanes and angles available from your bunker. This is the time to take note of bunkers that facilitate a pinch play. You and the other player on your team with the pinch shot must work together. Another important thing to keep in mind is that you may want to use the bunkers on the other side of the field as you advance. In this particular game plan the primary objectives are A5, B5, A3, and B3. A5 should be taken by the fastest tape runner. The back player, A1, has found a good shooting lane that cuts off the right side of the field. This lane cuts between bunkers and will be called Zone.

1. The objective for A1 is to eliminate player B3 at the break of the game. The objective for the players on the right side of the field is to eliminate player B5.

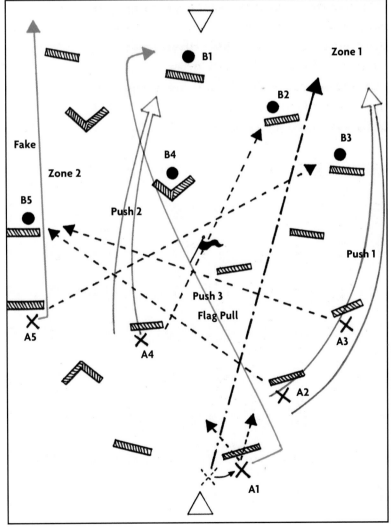

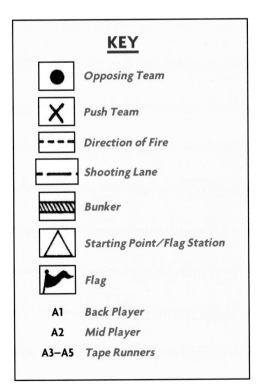

KEY

●	*Opposing Team*
X	*Push Team*
- - -	*Direction of Fire*
— ▪ —	*Shooting Lane*
▨▨▨	*Bunker*
△	*Starting Point/Flag Station*
🚩	*Flag*
A1	*Back Player*
A2	*Mid Player*
A3–A5	*Tape Runners*

2. Players B1 and B4 are not much of a factor in this game plan. As the back players signal, player A5 runs down the tape line. If player B5 is still in the game, A5 should eliminate him as he passes. A5 continues to run to the back corner of the field. This will cause the opposing team to turn in panic toward A5. It should be noted that if A5 had been eliminated prior to the signal, A4 would fill in. This is called a fake. A5 will most likely be hit performing this move. If he isn't, the opposing team has a huge problem. Timing is essential for this to work. Once A5 has begun his run, A2 and A3 should take advantage of the commotion and push the opposite side of the field. If the game plan has worked they should be able to eliminate some of the opposing team by shooting them in the back. Their primary objective would be to eliminate players B3, B2, and B1 in that order. A2 and A3 have now turned the remaining opposing players toward their side of the field. A4 should leave after A2 and A3. He should be advancing up the same side of the field as A5. His main objective is to eliminate player B4 and anyone else who remains. A1 follows A4 up the field. He should cross centerfield, picking up the flag as he advances. If the other players have done their job, all that is left for A1 to do is to hang the flag. This game plan incorporates four separate pushes. It is designed to keep the opposing team off balance. If it is executed well, the opposing team will be eliminated before they know what hit them. This is a very aggressive game plan. It is not simple to execute. If one player is too early (or late), the game plan may disintegrate leaving the opposing team with the upper hand.

Shooting Lanes

Shooting lanes should be chosen during field walking. The basic idea is to find a bunker on the opponent's side of the field that is key to their

game plan. Then find a way to eliminate the player who plans on getting into that bunker. The ideal shooting lane is a line of fire devoid of obstacles. The line of fire should drop the paint into the opposing player's running lane. In this example, player A1 shoots for Zone 1 dropping a line of paint into the path of B2 and B3. Mid player A2 stops half way to his bunker and fires into Zone 2, hoping to eliminate B3. This means that player B3 must cross zone 2 shooting lanes. This technique is used to increase the chances of eliminating a key player. Once B2 and B3 are in their bunkers (or eliminated), A1 and A2 need to take cover in their bunkers. Example 2 (shown in red) depicts 2 players firing in

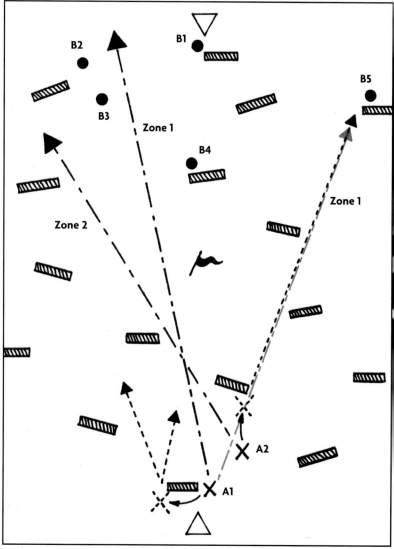

the same lane. This should only be done for an extremely key bunker. Player B5 must cross a firing lane with twice as much paint traversing it. This choice of firing lanes increases the chances of eliminating player B5. Hit or miss, A1 and A2 should get into their bunkers after B5 has passed the firing lane.

Keep in mind that shooting lanes are a great tool. They are not, however, foolproof. There is a certain amount of luck involved. This is a skill-based plan that should be practiced like any other. The back player using the lane needs to get a feel for the appropriate height to aim for. One trick to try is to aim at hip height at the entrance to the bunker. Even if the player comes in low he will usually not be below that point.

—MS

New Players' Guide to Cover

"Work your bunker." "Get angles from your bunker." "Slide out of your cover."

What does it all mean?

Cover is … "Anything that protects or shields from harm, loss, or danger."

In paintball, anything between you and an opponent that will stop, disable or render useless a fired paintball is considered "cover."

There are two basic types:

1. "Hard" cover includes medium- to large-sized trees, rocks, and bunkers.
2. "Soft" cover, like grass, small trees, and shrubs.

Both types serve the same function, but you'll learn to use them differently.

Let's tackle hard cover first. Virtually all speedball fields are exclusively hard cover. Meaning there's a very solid object between you and the other guys. Big trees, rocks, and bunkers are solid cover from incoming paintballs. Some fields have berms, hills, and other terrain features that qualify as hard cover.

A berm is a ledge or space between the ditch and parapet in a fortification.

Most paintball buildings are usually about 2 meters in length and width. (That's about 7 feet for you Americans.) This makes them about 4 square meters of doom that I can exploit as an attacker!

Look at buildings as traps rather than as fortresses, and a world of attack possibilities will open up to you!

LIKE "THE DEATH STAR," BUILDINGS HAVE THEIR WEAKNESSES

Personally, when I'm approaching a building filled with paintball players, I know that I have an enormous advantage. First of all, buildings are not mobile. (If they are, they're called tanks.) This fact alone might scare you out of buildings for the rest of your paintball career. (You shouldn't let it, but more on that later.) Once inside a building (especially if there's more than one entrance), this is where you're going to stay. Sure, you can move around inside there, but you're still on the same piece of real estate.

Stuck in a building like a roach in a roach motel.

You can't flank in a building, unless it's an unusually long one. You can't really crawl. You can't do much in there other than defend perhaps 3 angles that the openings and the doorways will allow. Defenders tend to exploit this to a fault. They will defend those angles with their last paintball.

You can't win a game based on mobility by taking and defending a building!

As an attacker, exploit the isolation and siege mentality of a building defender. The fact that most of a building is impenetrable also means that its occupants have substantial blind spots. It also means that their ability to hear what you're doing on the outside is easily compromised, because in many cases the buildings are echo chambers; a few

shots against those walls while you're moving will make it hard for them to hear where you're going. Once you know the angles the building allows its inhabitants, you can use different angles they can't cover. If this sounds simple, that's because it is. You just need to be patient, perceptive, and decisive in your attack.

A building can be worked through or over if need be. For example, you can dedicate one shooter to a building and basically stop everyone in that building from poking their heads out. This tactic plays out in the following manner.

If three guys are inside a building structure, they have limited fields of view. They can't all poke out of the same window without missing something and/or becoming a huge target. Here's what you do. Place one player near the front of the building and have him shoot it up a little to make noise along the building's sides. I call this "knocking," because you're just making them nervous instead of trying to eliminate them.

The next move is a flanking maneuver exploiting the limited visibility of the building's occupants. If you can manage to put paint in the vicinity of or through the openings, you'll make the occupants sloppy and nervous. Before you know it, you'll have cleared the building, because they won't have seen or heard you come right up on top of them. Or, if all of their players are in the building, why bother

to take it? If you can ignore the building, grab the flag while they're tied up with a well entrenched front shooter who has a great shot at their escape door.

Tactics for loners who must take a building

What if you're alone? Well, the principles are the same, but in this case I'll tie 'em up infinitely by shooting and maneuvering while they're ducking down from my shots. Either that or I'll just put paint into a hole until some poor dude pokes his head up to see what's happening. Poof—instant elimination!

WHAT BUILDINGS ARE USEFUL FOR

I've said some harsh things about paintball buildings. Clearly, buildings are the bane of those who misuse them.

On the other hand, buildings can be helpful to those who use them appropriately. For example, they should be used as cover. Despite everything I've just said, I'd like to remind the reader that buildings are more than just four walls.

When I'm using a building for cover I try to stay on the outside of it as long as I can. In this case, it's used like any bunker with the exception that the holes can line up to form a smaller hole for opponents to shoot through. I can shoot through easily, whereas my opponents can't.

I'll also back away from the building, and use it as a normal bunker that way. Buildings offer the opportunity to become invisible to my opponents. I only use this as a last resort, however. Or I use it as part of my tactical plan. Either way, using a building must serve a concrete purpose for the team.

When you enter a building, you're making a commitment.

Sometimes you'll be making a whole game commitment, because you'll end up in an inescapable hot zone. Of course, if your objective is to make your opponents focus on you, this can work to your team's advantage. If you're not doing anything for your team, you're not doing your job. Too many defenders forget that, and they get eliminated or they simply don't get involved in the game.

After diving into a building, it's important to keep your ears open for teammates' communications and to make your shooting count for something. Like any bunker, you have to work it. Buildings need to be worked harder because you don't have all the openings a bunker provides. Tunnel vision is easier to slip into from inside a building; if the window faces forward, you tend to look forward. Work a building's entryways the same way you work its windows and its cracks. Stay on your toes, or you'll get trampled point blank.

You really need to have a lot of team support for your building players. You need mobile people on the outside of the building to prevent flankers from taking your position. You also can make yourself a 'distraction' so that your teammates shoot the guys fixated on eliminating you. If you lie in a building, they can't touch you. But they'll keep trying because they think they can, and your teammates will just keep getting eliminations.

In January 1998, I played at an outdoor speedball field in Florida that had a few buildings in the center. During one game, I made a very bold move and made the center building. I took a few shots from the outside and realized that my team needed a gun a few feet forward. So I went into the building.

ANDREW: Cool.

CHUCK: You're down a foot or two below the line of sight and you usually have creek banks on both sides. People just don't expect to see you wading down a creek that's got a foot or a foot and a half of water in it.

One of the things that's interesting about hiding, and I tell new players this all the time, is that you always find bunkers and trees and log piles and fox holes. Everybody thinks those are the ideal places to hide. I disagree. I want to hide where somebody is not going to look for me, and those places are intrinsically suspicious.

I strive for a shooting lane that provides me an effective, defensible, dangerous position to work from. That's what I try to do.

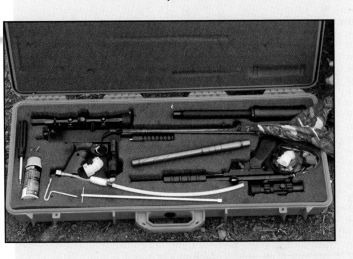

ANDREW: And a dangerous, defensible position to work from would be...

CHUCK: I need shooting lanes, I need to feel confident that I'm going to see everything, that I'm going to encounter targets. I need to position myself strategically where I can help my team because I'm not always out there to play for myself. I want to be somewhere useful. I want to encounter other players and I want to effectively engage them and paint them or send them in another direction.

ANDREW: What shooting stance do you prefer as a sniper? Would you use the prone shooting position?

CHUCK: Almost never! I never lay down on my belly. First of all, I've got a pump, and if you lay down in a prone position it makes it harder to work the pump. When you play, you should move very little or not at all. When you do move, move steadily with smooth movements. When things go south, and you decide that you have to move, be definitive. Move really fast! If you're laying down on your belly, you can't get the heck out of there if you need to. So I always play kneeling or standing.

Some players, especially those coming from military backgrounds, plop down on their belly as soon as they get into a fight. I just eat them up. Shooting from prone position may work in other situations, but when you're playing paintball, it's not completely effective.

ANDREW: I notice you play with a scope.

CHUCK: Yes I do play with a scope. While I'm picking my targets I keep the yellow lens cover down. If I take a hit in the lens of the scope then I've lost my targeting system. Just before I take my shot I pop up the lens cover and set my sights on the target, giving me a clear field of view.

It's a straight four power (4X) scope. When I originally put it on the gun, I had some problems with it because it made my targets appear so close that I tended to undershoot them. But I've just taught myself to play with it and now it's just part of my equipment and second-nature to me.

I can shoot like most people do: looking down the barrel and shooting. My pump gun doesn't have an auto-trigger so my rate of fire doesn't even begin to approach a semi's rate of fire. A Tracer or a Phantom with an auto-trigger can fire faster, but maybe not as accurately.

ANDREW: What shooting gear do you bring to the field with you?

CHUCK: I have my Bud Orr Sniper and I have

my backup gun, a Phantom that I played with full-time several years ago. It's a good gun, shoots just as straight and just as far as the Sniper. I play with the Sniper because I like its heft.

I bring a couple of extra barrels and a couple of extra elbows. It's really important to have the right size elbows. A couple of squeegees, some gun oil, a gunsmith screwdriver for making adjustments on the guns. Spare parts, o-rings, various bits and pieces for the guns.

ANDREW: Tell me a little bit about your dress and camouflage. What kinds of things determine your choice of camo?

CHUCK: There are so many patterns out there. You have to have an artist's eye to be able to critically regard the terrain that you're going to play in, and then select the camouflage pattern that you think will be most effective. I have snow camo, I have camo for the summertime, and I have camo for every season in between.

In the wintertime when there's snow on the ground, I have some white coveralls with some branch lines on them that are actually meant to be tree camouflage. I found that up here in the woods, where there's tons of angular branch features with a

white background, such camouflages are very effective. I can almost disappear.

In the Fall, if it rains, the color of the leaves darkens. I have a camouflage pattern that's called Fall Foliage that is a very effective pattern in conditions like that. Like I said, I'm a hunter and an outdoorsman and a paintball player all in one. My investment in all this equipment makes sense.

I wear hand coverings and face coverings. For most people in the woods, those are the most noticeable parts of the body. And again, since human eyes are set up to see movement, concealing your face and hands is rather important.

ANDREW: Do you have any memorable experiences as a sniper you can share?

CHUCK: Here's a classic. I coached a player, Rob, a couple of years ago. He wanted to become a sniper. At one point in the game, he hid in the top of a blown down tree and four players on the opposing team walked right past him! He and I and some of our other players were working together to set up an ambush. Everybody has to contribute to make those work. Our contribution was to engage the approaching players and have them concentrate on us. Then Rob just raised up out of the blown down tree top (he was fifteen yards behind them) and they were all four lined up with their backs to him and he just went to work on them. It was beautiful. That's how I like to play. It was a most enjoyable success.

ANDREW: That's great. How about yourself? Ever been ambushed?

CHUCK: It happens to the best of us. I like to match wits with people, to out-think them. People are just like deer, very much creatures of habit. It's

DEFENSE

Not enough has been written about defense in paintball, and the reasons are apparent. Very few of us think of playing defense in paintball as either a glamorous or enjoyable experience. Indeed, most players' idea of defense is to hang back and shoot anything not friendly as it comes back to the flag station.

But this isn't defense, it's a siege mentality. Bona fide paintball defense is a multifaceted position that's all about controlled aggression. If you understand the dimensions of paintball defense, you will think twice before leaving it out of your game plan.

The idea of defense that true paintball jedi should employ involves channeling your desire to win into preventing the other team from winning.

What am I talking about? Soon, it will all make sense. Most paintball teams are very concerned with taking ground fast, slamming a tape, and being very aggressive in their actions. But a team has to balance that with some kind of defensive capability, and not in the classical "Old School" sense. Paintball is becoming a game of players with positional strengths. Once you accept that proposition, exploring the possibilities of defense becomes more interesting.

First off, let me define paintball-style defense. Defensive players are those on the team attempting to stop the opposition from scoring points. Eliminations, flag hangs, first pulls—all of these are points that can be prevented with a good defense, and not just in tournaments either. If you play for fun, you can play a solid defense and win with it.

What makes a good defender? The mindset of a defender is a combination of fierce pride and spartan commitment. "You're not getting my flag. You're not shooting my crawler. You're not getting that bunker. Not on my field!" Sounds a lot like an aggressor, yes? The difference is that as a defender, your "aggressive" goal requires actively preventing *them* from attaining *their* goals. Hence the phrase, **Controlled Aggression**.

A fat wallet helps. Defense isn't cheap, you can shoot a ton of paint on "D."

So what's the purpose of defense? I've broken it down to four basic categories:

1. **Positional Defense**—Holding a single piece of real-estate with everything you have.

2. **Prevent Defense**—Also known as "Sitting". Playing solely to deny the opposing team from shooting your team or achieving their goals.

3. **Reserve Defense**—Staying in the back with the eventual goal of becoming an attacking player in a later stage of the game.

4. **Team Defense**—Playing the backfield to aid your forward players.

As a defensive player, you have to decide what style is best for your team and its goals and adapt on the fly. In a big game, it means holding the fort. In a hyperball tournament, you may prevent the other team from advancing and scoring points. In your rec-ball weekend, it could mean being the last line of defense because the corned beef sandwich you ate for lunch just isn't sitting right and running is more than you can handle. *Remember the team goal is important, and so is not barfing during a game.*

Paintball is, and always will be, a team sport.

Defense falls into two broader styles—"Passive" and "Aggressive." As the names suggest, the two styles reflect two different trains of thought, but one overall goal: denying points and positions to the opposing team. There's a general stereotype here for the two styles. "Rec-Ball" players are 'passive' defenders, whereas tournament players are 'active' defenders. Tournament teams leave no players back, but rec-players always do. Yes, it's a stereotype, but it's almost always true. As in everything else, there's a time to be passive, and other times when being aggressive is necessary. Learning the rhythm of the game is very important. It's key to know when you need to act, to feel the appropriateness of doing something. With this in mind, let's go into a little more detail on the four basic categories of defense.

Positional Defense is mainly a concern of passive defenders, mainly because it requires patience in the beginning and cunning when it hits the fan. Active defenders can use the principles of this to take and hold key bunkers and control zones from one spot on the field. Examples of this can be found mostly in big games where a flag station or a fort must be held. On tournament fields, situations arise wherein a defender holds the last few bunkers and tries to stop the offense.

Most positional defense originates in one location, and uses that location to fend off all aggressors. This is a very passive defense, and is very common in rec-play. From a position like this, you want to work around as in a typical bunker. But you have to keep your eyes open because you will more than likely be seeing more than one attacker and they have the maneuverability advantage and often greater numbers.

Aggressive Defense is about players having *zones of influence* that they can claim as their own. This is a very aggressive defense, because you as the defensive player are making the action happen and causing people to react to you. You're grabbing a section of field X by Y in size, staking a claim, and

putting up a sign that reads "No trespassers allowed." As a defender, it allows you to move around more and remain unpredictable. Slide forward to a position to stop them; scuttle to the other side of the bunker and shoot it up. While they're adjusting, move back a position and draw one into your barrel. Take him down and dive to another bunker. Scope out two bunkers you can dive between to make them wonder. If you can keep them guessing so they can't figure out where you are, they will hesitate to move up on you. My girlfriend calls this a "Field Mouse Defense" because it's what a field mouse does and, in her words, "What's more defensive than a field mouse?" Be elusive!

The Surprise Factor

You also want to have the element of surprise. You can accomplish this even if your enemy knows where you are. Consider the following scenario.

At the Ohio Bash, we had a position we had to hold for 5 more minutes so our team captain could touch the station for more points. I had a pump gun, and a few surprises. The team was laying paint heavily into the other team's attacking force. I put my body in front of our captain and began to pump paint to keep their heads down. I kept watching the time, knowing it wouldn't be long. With a minute before the call in, I grabbed a smoke grenade, popped the striker, and tossed it just over the lip of the hill.

It was a good throw, but the smoke wasn't thick enough for my liking. So I popped a red smoker with it and tossed it over the hill as well. "Hammer down!" I yelled. My teammates doubled their rate of fire, stopping our opponents' last minute push. Our captain touched the flag station, and we got our points and vacated the area. The opposing team wasn't expecting a smoke screen, and that stopped them long enough for our team to achieve our goal. This was Controlled Aggression exemplified.

Let it all hang out, but don't take unnecessary risks!

Prevent Defense

Related to positional defense, **prevent defense** uses similar means, but tends to be more useful in tournament settings. Simply put, you're preventing the other team from advancing instead of holding a position. For example, if the opposing team needs to eliminate five of your guys to advance, you fare better by sitting back and making them do the work. They get sloppy or nervous, and they get eliminated. Prevent defense is also easier than position defense because it's not zone oriented. It's more aggressive as well: you hide less and being mobile is emphasized.

I was in Chicago once, and had the opportunity to talk to some guys from Thunderstruck. They were telling me about a tournament field in Vegas some years ago in which they zoned out one bunker at extreme range down a main trail. One guy from the start would take three steps and start laying paint just over that bunker. He made three eliminations in the first two minutes. This is a perfect prevent defense. Other players on his team were making aggressive moves, but this one shooter made the plan work—*controlled aggression is where it's at!*

Most of your defense should be geared towards a "prevent" style. It's very flexible in response to what the other team is doing, but it's not just reactive. If you've done your job before the games start, you should have scoped out the bunkers your opposition is likely to see as advantageous. Dedicate a defense player to preventing them from getting in and/or using that position. Even if someone makes it in, rain paint on their heads so they won't even look up. Now *that's* effective prevention.

Delay Tactic

The other side to a prevent is a **delay tactic** in which you aren't stopping the other team as much as you're stalling the inevitable or forcing them to deal with you. A good friend of mine calls this tactic "The Human Speedbump." We do this in big games all the time. The entire offense is getting routed hard, and we figure that they need a few more seconds to get away. So we stop hard behind a tree and start shooting at the attackers. They always stop to return fire, and we always get eliminated. But we always get our teammates a few hundred more feet of running room in the trade, and they can be more effective. You may also have seen a tournament player crash a front bunker and just hug it. The opposing team is forced to deal with that player, because he's a threat in their path. You may not consider this a defensive maneuver until you realize this one player is stopping the entire other team from pushing a side by just sitting there. Again, this is controlled aggression—doing just enough to stop the 'bad guys' and help the 'good guys' without getting hit.

Reserve Player Defense

The **Reserve player tactic** is a different defense mostly used in recreational play. The general idea is to hang back and wait to see what the opposing team does. Your time interval for this is up to you. For example, I've been playing a lot of speedball style games lately (no deer ticks, and none of this hiding stuff...). Earlier this summer I played at a field in Wisconsin that was preparing for a tournament, so the speedball field was all nice and dolled up. We were also playing the older speedball style of

"Tiger Stripe" fall into this category, but for a different reason. You see, the human eye is lazy. When we scan for opponents, we scan horizontally. Aggressive camouflage, like Tiger Stripe, encourages the eye to "slide over" it. There's a few other camouflages like this. US Woodland was actually created for a European military theater by the United States government. Tiger Stripe was originally made for the Vietnam conflict, but was modified slightly for paintballers. You don't want to know how much the Australian government spent on developing Auscam, but it's the best stuff for hiding in Australia that I've found.

Passive camouflage works in a different way; it's made to convince the brain it's part of the foreground, and totally natural. This would include Advantage, Realtree (and it's derivatives), Mossy Oak, and so on. Each of these types is perfect for specific uses. "Advantage" looks like the forest floor, while "Realtree" looks like a tree. These camouflages started as hunting patterns. They are supposed to enable a hunter to stand in front of a tree to get a better shot. That's why they try to be photo-realistic. They're not really meant for other terrain. In their elements, these highly specialized camouflages are excellent.

Then there's a third kind of camouflage, which I call "Weirdo-Flage." These types fit mostly into the "Aggressive" camouflage category. They include, but aren't limited to, JT, Scott, Renegade or Venomwear printed jerseys, Splash clothing. Any of the "Non-Camo" stuff also falls into this category. The idea behind these patterns is simply to bring paint-

ball into the 'mainstream'. Paintball garb as fashionable accessory...you get the picture. They work toward that end, and, occasionally, as partial camouflage. I love the guys who wear off-the-shelf JT Jerseys. Big, juicy white target in center of their chest and on their forearms. Easy target from across the field. Love it.

Some of the non-camo works, but not as well as true camouflage. If you're wearing it to look like a team, cool. If you're wearing it as a true camo... well... umm... yeah...

Whatever you're wearing, the golden rule of camouflage is not to move. The human eye is lazy, but it's also naturally drawn to motion. Motion is perceived as something worth watching.

Paintball players, of course, have to move. Given that fact, note that "Aggressive" patterns allow you more freedom of movement than "Passive" patterns. Aggressive patterns aren't specific to one spot or terrain, and allow you to take a "camouflaged" position anywhere in a broad spectrum of places. If you're wearing a Realtree and you're lying down, it doesn't "look" right and you're more apt to be spotted. A "Tiger Stripe" looks more appropriate in any given place you stop.

As a player, you can also use different patterns in different terrain. I have a set of Realtree I've used in the desert. It worked well. This isn't brain surgery, people. The key is simply to match your camouflage as accurately as possible to your surroundings. I've seen pictures of UK players in Tiger Stripe in which the green just blares out against a brown background; we're talking total absence of greenage on the ground level. I've made boo-boos like this before, mostly in my paintball youth. And if it happens by mistake these days, I just change my outlook on the game and adapt. I'll look for colors where I'm close to blending in and go from there.

Camouflage—All or Nothing!

Use a visor on your goggles or at least a hat brim. Goggle flare is a dead giveaway to your position. Don't use chrome or bright, splashy stuff that may glare as well. Matte Black is still your best bet for color. Wear a full mask. Skin tones aren't nature tones and will give you away. Better yet, paint your mask for camo colors or mottle it somehow to break up the "Black Blob" on your face. My favorite trick is hiding your brightly colored armband by burying your arm into a tree or the ground and using your body as a "cloak" over it.

BEHAVING INVISIBLE

There's a time and a place for battle cries and open charges down the middle, but this ain't one of 'em!

Wait your opponent out. They panic when nobody is shooting at them. Take your time and you'll absolutely freak 'em out.

You don't need cool camos or anything like that to hide, however. I could be wearing stark white, and you won't see me if I'm totally behind hard cover (see the Cover chapter). It's that easy. Let's say I'm wearing a really bright jersey and I've got a bright red paintgun. If I'm trying to hide, I'll get behind a rock, a dirt berm, or a hill. Anything I can put my whole body behind relative to an enemy position will hide me.

Nature is one big free camouflage factory!

Use Reference Points and the World Around You

Having a reference point is good as well. I'll often use cover from one angle, knowing that the other team or another player will be coming from that or another angle and crossing my barrel. I can expose myself to one side if I know that side is *safe*. That's

why I run the tape as often as I do, I can expose that whole flank as I wait for you to walk into my dot-sight. Pop, "HIT", Bingo. Thank you.

Terrain is a big part of fieldcraft. Your fieldcraft skills come from learning how to use what's ahead of you and see what's to the side of you. Lining up trees to conceal your movement toward your opponents is always a good idea. You can't plan on things like shadows, wind, and so on to mask your movement. You just have to do it.

But when it all falls together, you have to recognize it for what it is. If I'm stalking a tape (either by crawl or by crouch), I'm constantly aware of my surroundings. I'm looking ahead for the clearest line in the path that requires minimal effort and noise. Leaves are bad, dirt is good. If I have a choice between twigs or dried leaves, I'll take the twig route. I can push twigs out of my way quieter and faster than I can leaves by just dragging my hand along them and not lifting my knees too far.

I'm always listening to the wind. When it picks up, I move. When it dies down, I slow or stop. I listen for airplanes, cars, trucks, trains, people shooting in the center... anything that makes enough noise to mask my movement.

Moves are made quickly and deliberately, and planned 2 steps ahead when possible. The thought process is: "Big Tree to fort. Fort to spool. Spool to shrubs."

I'm always looking ahead. I'm also looking down the field to where opponents *should* be hiding. I can't predict everything, but if I'm coming up on a big tree or an outcropping of barrels, odds are someone is either in there or wants to be. *I'm looking through cover for background shadows.* If I don't see any light behind twigs or shrubs, it's either a rock, a tree, or a player.

Sounds play a very important role, too. Especially nature sounds. Most things in nature that produce noisy sounds will stop when something big comes by and scares them. If the birds and crickets stop chirping, someone spooked them and you should get ready. In some cases, an animal may start making a lot of noise if you approach. Listen for any and all audible changes; they're the best early warning system you'll have in the wild.

A bit of fieldcraft also goes into using nature to fool people. These are old school tricks, but they're still good. Here are some examples from my experience. I'm lying on the ground while two guys are looking for me. They know I'm out there, but not sure where. With one foot I'll wiggle a small tree or a thick shrub away from me. That will get their attention long enough for me to come up and take 'em out. There's also the "Throw a rock away from you so it makes noise over there" trick, but I stopped doing that out of fear of pelting a ref or well-hidden player. You'd be well advised to throw only relatively light things. I've also been stalking, been spotted, and swayed matching the tree in front of me for movement. The player looked away, and I got moving at the flag. (I was able to get the flag, and not make a single elimination that game.) Then there's the 'ballsy' approach. Someone thinks they see me, and they open a barrage at me. I don't flinch or move. After a few moments, they stop shooting. Why? Nothing shot back, obviously nobody's there. One burst later, they're gone.

CLAIM THIS LOST ART AND PUT IT IN YOUR GAME

To a paintball player who uses fieldcraft, tactical possibilities are virtually infinite. I've crawled through a path with no cover in front of me and made it, and I've sat in front of a tree and remained unseen. But if you think this is all there is to know, you're wrong.

I talked to a friend of mine; he plays in ratty old BDU's, uses a pump gun, and wears no mask. He's one of my favorite wire players, because he can just vanish after taking a guy out and pop up thirty paces to the right of where he just was. He's very good. When I started writing this piece, I asked him for help. "Sure!" he said. "Who's gonna read it?" I said new players and tournament competitors. "No way, man!" he said. "I'm not gonna tell 'em all my secrets! I've earned *some* advantage over them!"

I agree. Some secrets are meant to be discovered rather than shared. Besides, I learned from the best. I can't let out all our trade secrets. Ninja Union Local 151 won't let me.

—RR

"ALL-AMERICAN" THINGS YOU CAN DO TO IMPROVE YOUR GAME

"When you attack, you want to attack from the highest heights of heaven. And when you defend, you want to defend from the deepest resources of the earth."
LAO TZU, THE ART OF WAR

BILL GARDNER: First, we'll talk about individual tactics, then we'll talk about squad tactics and team tactics. When I say individual tactics, I mean aspects of the game that improve the individual's play.

And a lot of this comes down to the simple things. For example, there are different ways to load. Obviously, if you stick your elbow out, it becomes a target. You need to learn how to load with your elbow tucked in. These are the little things that make the difference between winning and losing.

You have to develop certain basic skills. First, you have to learn to shoot. You also have to realize that you're not going to be afforded the opportunity to just aim and slowly pull the trigger. You need to work on your snap shooting—the ability to stay within a bunker, then snap out and shoot a target, and then get back behind cover quickly.

Almost every player that achieves any level of skill in this sport gets comfortable with shooting a target at 40 yards or so with a quick snap and a couple of shots. So, from an individual standpoint, you must work on accuracy.

Then, there are bunker tactics—the ways you work a bunker. During a game you often end up behind some structure, either a speed ball bunker or a stick bunker in the woods.

Never look from the same place twice in a row. You bring your head up at the same place every time, and the other guy watches your head come up at the same spot, two times before. So he aims at that spot. As you bring your head up again the paint is on its way, and you're wet before you know where it came from. So learn to peek around left, take two shots, then peek around right and take two shots. Keep your opponent off guard.

Paintball is an aural game, too. You can hear your opponent's gun go off. You can hear paint fly through the air; it whizzes. So, you can and should use your ears to determine when to come up and where to shoot.

ADAM GARDNER: People get shot just because they stay up too long. They want to watch their paint fly and then yell about it. Remember, you can call for a paint check just as effectively from behind a bunker. You saw the ball far enough on it's path that you have a pretty good idea of whether you were on line or weren't. If you didn't get him, you can adjust.

You want to come up, take your shots and immediately duck down, Inexperienced players watch their paint fly through the air as if that's the best part of the game. When they get a hit, they freak out and make themselves an easy target.

BILL: Blind shooting is another excellent tactic. If you're playing in a wooded field, look beyond your opponent for reference points you can zero in on from a better, protected position, and put paint in that direction. For example, get a fix on a branch right over the guy's head. You have a good chance of getting a hit and you minimize your risk of being shot. That's the beauty of blind shooting.

Knowing the Game, Playing to Win

I have always believed that understanding leads to success. Many players play paintball without ever truly understanding the underlying concepts, which is the only way that a person can advance in this sport. As a result of this, many people misinterpret what happens during a game and learn nothing from watching them. Case in point...

After my team, Aftershock, won a game at the World Cup in Orlando, I heard one kid tell his friend, "Oh yeah, you should have seen them. They just mowed the other team down. Aftershock just got up and went at'em. They smoked'em, dude." He was referring to Aftershock winning the game impressively. But he had completely missed the true nature of what had happened. He seemed to be implying that the win was wholly attributable to Aftershock's attack; it wasn't. He couldn't differentiate between what looked dramatic and what had actually transpired.

Witnessing a team dominate and demolish the opposition, without a doubt one of the most exciting and memorable aspects of paintball, sticks in the mind because it is so dynamic. But it does not tell the whole story. Not by a longshot.

The bottom line is that if you want to progress in this sport, you need to learn how to understand what is going on!

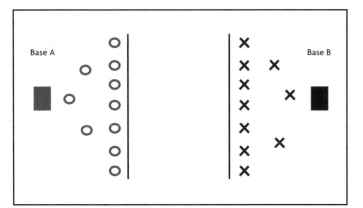

The above illustration is a rough guide to what 99% of tournament paintball teams do when they position themselves at the start of the game. If you look at any tournament game, you will see each team run out to initial positions on the first third of the field, as shown above. The teams will sit in these positions and duke it out until one side gets a few more kills than the other. At that point, the prevailing team will make their move. Only after a significant number of eliminations have been made does the end game unfold. Obviously, the team that gets the most kills in this part of the game normally wins.

Paintball can be broken down, like chess, into three parts: the opening, middle, and the end.

THE OPENING GAME

This is best described as the part of the game where your teammates run out to their primary cover points: the bunkers or trees that you have selected to be your first stopping points.

Now this part of the game, unlike the other two, is completely under your control.

Before the game, your team should have agreed on a selection of bunkers that were not only the

safest to attain, but also provided the best angles for eliminating the opposition.

When the game starts, you should know where you and your teammates are headed, and the path you will use to run to your primary position.

Your team's entry into primary positions should be accomplished without any losses if you have done your prep work correctly.

Having control is important because if you control proceedings then you can predict outcomes (e.g., the victories you aspire to). Without control, you are a hostage to fortune. Luck will smile on you one day and not the next.

With one hundred percent control, you can do whatever you want with no real interference from the other team. But once you get in this position, the middle part of the game begins, and this is where paintball games are won and lost.

THE MID GAME

Ninety-nine percent of paintball games at tournaments follow similar patterns. Both teams run out to their respective primary positions and start firing their guns. As soon as the mid game progresses, people begin to walk off the field.

The stronger team starts picking off the weaker team one by one. This is where the real damage is done. The determinant of who will actually win the game is generally who gets the most kills off the basic line format. This is one of the fundamentals of tournament play.

All tournament teams try to play this way. They run out to their positions, which roughly extend across the width of a field in a line. In this way, all the bases are covered. Both defensive and attacking capabilities can be optimized across all areas of the field.

The basic layout of a field is the length of it divided into three sections. The first third line is where each team lines up. The middle third line of the field is the *killing ground*, and the final third line is where (from your perspective as a player) the opposition resides.

The Mid-Game is the Pivotal Phase

As I alluded to earlier, the perspective of the side line observer is limited because the truly decisive and key eliminations are achieved immediately before the *exciting* finale. Indeed, the reality is that by the time you see five or six tournament players get up and run down the last vestiges of the opponents' defense, the most decisive part of the game is already over. A controllable end game results from a successful mid-game.

> Since the mid game is so important, what can we do to make sure that it's successful?

Technique is the answer. If you are better than your opposition technically, then the killing ratio will be in your favor. If not, more of your team members will be eliminated and you will lose control of the end game. Lost control means defeat. Period.

> Paintball can appear very complex to many people when it is actually very simple. Once you understand the underlying concepts of it, everything makes sense.

There are no secrets in Paintball; everything is common sense.

THE END GAME

After a successful mid game, the end game should be yours. You began the game in control of your primary positioning. You used your technical prowess to acquire a high killing ratio, which left your opponents at a numeric disadvantage. Now you have control. But it isn't over yet; you still have to take advantage of your supremacy.

Almost everyone has heard of heroic last stands

from players who have killed five or six incoming players alone. It happens, but it shouldn't.

Superiority in numbers should mean victory, but there are exceptions when a field bias will sometimes confer an advantage to the team with fewer players. Not everything always goes exactly as planned in the end game. Sometimes the disadvantaged team wins. This sport is inherently unpredictable, but you must give yourself the best possible chance for success.

These are the basic concepts behind the game, but in order to increase your chances of winning, you must have an idea of the other available styles and strategies.

PLAYING STYLES

There are three basic playing styles in paintball: **defensive**, **technical**, and **aggressive**.

The Technical Style

Historically, the All-Americans exemplify the *technical* approach.

They sit on their line format and eliminate the other team's members with their superior techniques throughout the entire game.

As you watch an All American's game, you will notice a procession of their opponents toward the dead box for no reason other than that the All Americans shot them first. The trick is to do it consistently. That's what they do. If you want this to be your style, then you need to become an extraordinary sharp-shooter, drill regularly, and practice patience.

The Defensive Style

One of the reasons for playing a defensive game is to counter-attack the other team's offensive attacks. It is not very accepted on the tournament circuit because it is seen as a way of compensating for lack of skill and aggression.

Another reason for playing defensively is when the opposing team is believed to be better than your own. It's safer to move only when you are attacked instead of making an offensive move and opening yourself up to trouble.

Only a few teams use this strategy, but I won't mention them, since they might be insulted. So I won't mention Bob Long's Ironmen... but they are getting better! (Just kidding guys!)

The Aggressive Style

This is the most exciting and difficult way to play. It occurs when your team hits the wall of the opposing team, which only happens after significant eliminations have been made. Only two or three teams play this way: Aftershock, four-time World Cup champions, and Bob Long's Ironmen of 1991 to 1994, who were the greatest aggressive team of all time. They attacked with a series of line assaults that could and did break every defense.

KNOWING AND PRACTICING ARE DIFFERENT THINGS

Teams generally acquire their style by default, rather than design, which is a direct consequence of who is on their team. Conservative members play defensively, while eager and slightly crazy members play aggressively. The technical components of each style need to be molded to fit with the technical capabilities of each team. Those who are masterful paintball technicians experience paintball at its most exciting and rewarding. If that's your goal, you are aiming high, and better start practicing now. And now that you know what you have to do, you have no excuses.

—PR

More Than Just A Game

THE REWARDS OF PLAYING PAINTBALL

Jerry Braun Puts Paintball in Perspective

As you have seen, paintball is a game, a sport, a business, an escape, a regimen, an avocation, a corporate training device, a bonding experience, and an all around good time. And still, I would contend, paintball is more than the sum of its parts.

Something about paintball gives a great deal to those who play it. Paintball provides a structure within which players of all ages, backgrounds, physical make-ups, and beliefs can experience the thrill of victory. Its rules are simple and winning is accessible. That's especially important to young people.

Paintball's greatest value comes from what it does for young players. Those who never made the first squad of little league baseball, pee-wee football, or local soccer leagues, who often had to sit on the bench in frustration and embarrassment, can participate and excel in this game. They can score a key elimination, make a sacrifice that helps their team win, and hang the flag to win the game.

In paintball, the recognition, support, and congratulations young people receive from peers build a self-esteem few other activities can foster. To children and their parents, this is where paintball becomes more than just a game.

Travis Jenks takes the flag in front of a cheering crowd at Skyball 1999.

Children who are particularly talented at this game have access to ever increasing levels of difficulty, all the way up to amateur and professional leagues. There are no upper limits for those who seek an extremely challenging competitive experience in this up-and-coming sport.

The game nurtures communication skills, promotes values such as honesty, fair play, teamwork, and goal setting. It also introduces young people to the experience of being decisive, taking risks, and learning from the consequences of their actions. All of this occurs in a safe format and family-friendly atmosphere. In all of these ways, paintball builds character.

Paintball flourishes because it gives so much to its participants in so many different ways. It is an activity that has yet to reach its peak of popularity and its future seems limitless!

Living His Dream

Diagnosed with a rare form of Hodgkins Disease at the age of 16, Travis Jenks is making the most of every moment and taking nothing for granted. Travis seized the opportunity to play with and against the best players in professional paintball in Toronto at Skyball 1999, an international tournament. The Diggers and their owner Jerry Reilly, Operation Paintball, and Mare Island's owner, Matt Crandle, pitched in airfare for the Jenks family, and the Greater Bay Area Make-A-Wish Foundation made hotel arrangements.

Travis was especially grateful to play alongside his personal paintball hero, Bob Long of the Ironmen. This was not their first meeting. The two met initially at the Mare Island fields in California where Travis had his first chance to play with the Ironmen and the Diggers in a scrimmage planned for him by the Greater Bay Area Make-A-Wish Foundation.

> "I'd like to get a nice paintball marker and maybe go play with the Ironmen."

The entire paintball industry has rallied around Travis. Bud Orr donated a 98 Autococker and Bob Long gave him a prototype of his new electronic gun, the "Defiant," and a Signature Series Millennium. The Diggers pitched in with a Centerfire AutoMag (complete with Evolution hopper).

WHAT'S NEW AND WHAT'S HOT

BIGGER, BETTER, FASTER, MORE: TECHNOLOGY UPDATES

FROM NITROGEN TO ELECTROPNEUMATICS, NEW MARKERS ARE ROCKING THE FIELD

It would be hard to talk about the recent developments in paintball equipment without talking first about the recent advances in paintball marker technology. Over the past three years, many things have happened to improve the quality and availability of paintball guns on the market. Of note, the largest improvement has been in price.

You're Not Gonna Pay a Lot for This Marker!

On every level, from entry to tournament, the price of high-tech equipment has dramatically decreased. What was once considered unobtainable by the average paintball player has grown easier and cheaper to get. A lot of this has been due to an increase in supply as companies expand their resources and market their products to a larger audience. Probably the most dramatic price change has been in high-end electropneumatic paintball guns. For 50% of what you could spend on a high-end paintgun three years ago, you can buy a piece of equipment today that is equally competitive in terms of high-end performance. The Black Dragun, the BushMaster LCD, the Tippmann 98 Response, the Impulse, the Shocker, and the Spyder LCD are all examples of electropneumatic paintball guns that retail today for less than $600—something unheard of three years ago.

Several other goggles exist for paintball, and many are viable options, but it is important that whatever goggles you choose are ASTM certified. If they are not certified for paintball use, DO NOT WEAR THEM FOR PAINTBALL! It's that simple. As time goes on, goggles will become more sophisticated and become safer. But it will always be important that your goggles are made specifically for paintball games. Always check, and always check your lenses before you begin playing. Every time. You can't be too safe.

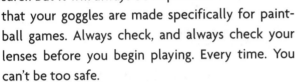

The guy on the right has a Warp Feed under his gun. (Courtesy Airgun Designs)

LOADERS GO ELECTRO

The description of the evolution of the paintball loader from the first edition of this book was complete up to the beginning of the millennium. In very recent times, however, the loader market has really come into the age of electronics.

A few years ago, the loader choices were basic. There were several companies making plastic tubes to hold paint before it went into the gun, but if you were a serious player, you used a Viewloader. More precisely, you used a motorized VL with a paddle to agitate the balls as you shot paint. The reason you did this was that nobody but Viewloader had figured out a system of loading paint from a cylinder to the elbow of a gun without the use of an electronic eye.

All of that changed just a few years ago. Some companies experimented with an "intelliport", a wire that went from the back of an electronic-style gun into a hopper telling it when to feed a ball. At the time, this left a majority of players high and dry, since many blowback semi-autos could not use this technology. Since then, however, with some experimenting and some radical designs, the choices that have become available are amazing.

Warped Minds Think Alike

But, first, one of the predictions we made in this book did come to pass: "force-feed" (see p. 193) was realized in Airgun Designs' Warp Feed. The Warp Feed is a box that can be mounted under the grip frame of any paintball gun. You then attach any kind of loader you like, and it sits to the side of the Warp Feed. The loader is no longer on top of the gun, and is no longer a target when it comes over the top of a bunker.

The Warp Feed box pushes paintballs from the loader into the gun with two discs that spin when there's no paint in the tube. This action pushes paint up from under the gun and into an elbow that already exists in the gun. Cutting-edge technology for the serious pro player.

The Warp Feed. (Courtesy Airgun Designs)

Welcome to the Game of Paintball

The Latest from Viewloader...

As for what loader the average player should use, as we said before, you have many options to match your needs. Viewloader is still making their impressive VL2000, but it's been improved over the years, and loaders are now available to meet a variety of needs. The standard 9-volt VL2000 is good for most users, feeding paint at 5-7 balls per second. For heavier shooters, a 12-volt model provides a larger paddle and faster response time. It feeds paint at an average of 10-12 balls per second.

The 12-volt model of the VL2000
(Courtesy JT USA)

Recently, Viewloader has made improvements to the basic Revolution system. They replaced the old plastic shell with polycarbonate for extra durability during impacts in close quarters. Viewloader also recently came out with an improved sensor for their clear and translucent loaders called the X-Board, which is less sensitive to light than the old circuit boards that came with VL2000s.

The X-Board sensor
(Courtesy JT USA)

...And Everybody Else

The VL system is patented, so the largest problem facing competitors has been the need for a new way to agitate paintballs in a loader. It took several years to do it, but many companies have finally come up with solutions.

Zap Paintballs recently came out with a loader called the Mach 404, which has the highest capacity out of all the new loaders: over 210 paintballs. Their system uses a central spindle that swings like a pendulum and agitates the paintballs. It works on vibration from your paint gun, agitating at a power relative to the vibrations it's receiving. If you give it a moderately hard tap with your hand, it will agitate the balls at the maximum speed, as compared to the gentler vibration of your gun when you shoot normally.

A more radical approach to loader technology came from Ricochet Engineering, who came up with a loader named the Ricochet-2K. This loader is radical in many ways, most obviously in its appearance, which is something between a stealth fighter and a spacecraft from a sci-fi movie. The Ricochet series was engineered not only to hold paint, but also to deflect paintballs that are coming in to your position. This is important since standard paintball rules say that a hit to the loader counts as an elimination.

The Ricochet series also uses a small switch in the feed neck to move the agitator fingers every

The Ricochet with digital timer/counter
(Courtesy Ricochet Development)

time a ball is fired. There are several models, from a bare-bones one to a fully tricked-out model with an easy to read ball counter and an on-loader timer.

In terms of speed, the fastest-feeding hopper on the market right now is arguably the HALO (Highly Advanced Loader Operation) from Odyssey products. It works like a high-speed egg counter, with a spinning disk to sling paintballs into the open feed neck. But, while it does feed paint very fast, the large size of the HALO may be a turnoff to many people.

With so many choices now available, the modern player can choose a loader to fit any playing style. A back player might need a loader that feeds faster, while a front player might need one that is smaller and more compact. As with all other gear, you can customize your loader to meet your own specific needs.

Some of the information on loaders came from http://www.warpig.com, Copyright Bill Mills

PODS, PACKS, AND PROGRESS

Although accessories, pods, and harnesses haven't undergone the same kind of dramatic technological evolution as guns, barrels, and loaders, there are still plenty of products out there to choose from. In recent years, most pods have held 145 paintballs, and the most recent innovations have made them even faster and more convenient to use.

The Snapp™ speed loader. (Courtesy Allen Paintball Products)

JT, for example, created the Slammer Pod system. These pods have a sliding opening that rides along the outside of the pod. When you push the pod into a "speed collar," it opens like a flower and pours paint into the end hopper. It's the fastest method of reloading made yet. It does have the disadvantage that the pods are never truly closed, so water can get into them. But, for raw speed, you can't beat it.

Other innovations along these lines came from Allen Paintball Products. Their Snapp™ Speed Loader is a pod with a tapered lip and a snapping cap. Among this system's many advantages is the fact that you don't need to buy a whole specialty system to go along with it. They have also developed a curved pod, which fits to the contour of the back and hugs the body when worn in a harness system.

Over the years, style has developed along with function. Planet, a company famous for its various high-end modified guns, has created loaders with a mirror-sheen finish in silver, purple, and a few other colors. In direct sunlight, these pods deflect harmful heat to help keep the paint cool, making reloads easier. But the main advantage is that they look really cool when you have an open harness to put them in.

Packing It In

Harnesses have changed more radically than pods in recent years, becoming more comfortable and easier to use. In some cases, manufacturers have gone back to ideas from the old days of paintball, with results that work as well today as they did

Slammer SpeedPods™ (Courtesy JT USA)

in the past. For example, Redz, who built the first truly comfortable pack based on a support belt, have updated their product with the largest breakthrough of the past few years: modular packs. A player can get a few styles of pack and easily interchange them on the basic belt pack depending on what style of game they're playing. If you need lots of paint, get a pack with more pouches. If you need less, get a pack with less. The modular nature makes this pack great for players who change position from game to game. Other manufacturers have made modular systems, too. Jacko makes a pack with zippers, so you can add or subtract sleeves to hold pods. Other companies make similar systems.

Redz also has been using an old idea of stacking tubes in a pyramid style to fit more pods in less space. They do this with a traditional pack, and then use elastic loops between the pods of an additional stack pack. Other companies like Planet and M-Class have been doing this as well. The idea originated back in the days of the 10 round tube harnesses, but has become a way to really carry more.

Flaming bones from Animal Paintball (Courtesy Animal Paintball)

Earlier in the book (see p. 179), we demonstrated how middle players can tape two pods together to carry them. M-Class now makes what they call a 'football', which is a neoprene sleeve that holds two pods for just this purpose. The advantages are very easy to see: no tape, no messes, and you can use any pods you like in them.

Other packs have specifically focused on comfort. JT and DYE have both made packs with a lot of back support in them. Both have a lumbar support, and both are rather comfortable to wear. JT made theirs to fit with the slam pods I mentioned earlier, but they will also fit any brand of pod you wish to use. Other companies like APP have also made more comfortable packs. And, as with all things wearable, it's all about your personal comfort.

FROM CAMO TO DAY-GLO: PAINTBALL FASHION COMES OUT OF HIDING

When this book first came out, paintball was going through a revolution in clothing as more and more events moved out of the woods and into arena settings. With camouflage becoming unnecessary, many players started to embrace the idea of brighter clothing that was made specifically for the paintball market. The paintball industry was more than happy to comply, and a lot of corporations that were previously not involved with paintball are now jumping in with both feet.

Today, you can find paintball jerseys to match any particular. You want dragons? Paintball Junkies. Prefer the flaming skeleton look? Animal Paintball. Something a little more solid in color? Smart Parts. Something you can wear in the woods? JT or Renegade. When this book first came out, there were a few choices, but not nearly as many as there are today!

And something a little more subtle from Smart Parts (Courtesy Smart Parts)

one on each side. And two large tubes—they look like vacuum cleaner tubes—come down to each side of the Vulcan gun. The gun itself is run by a cordless electric drill. And it shoots extremely fast. Top speed is around 50 rounds a second.

THE FUTURE OF TIPPMANN PAINTBALL

ANDREW: Let's talk about the future of paintball and Tippmann. Three years ago, the Model 98 was the hot item. Now we're looking at the A-5. Where do you see paintball three years hence?

DENNIS: It's hard to predict what's going to happen with the industry. It always surprises us; it keeps growing and growing. The sport will probably be quite a bit bigger if it keeps growing at the same rate.

The other thing we notice is that it seems like the technology has definitely slowed down since the beginning. In the beginning you couldn't design things fast enough. Now it's getting harder and harder to come up with new and better gun designs.

So I could see a lot of fine-tuning of the current equipment that's on the market. But I don't think there's a need for a lot more firepower. A lot of the tournaments are starting to limit, and obviously they don't allow full auto in most tournaments. Pretty much everyone is putting on a rule that semi-auto is the limit.

But they are allowing the electric triggers, which allow you to shoot very quickly in semi-auto. So I don't see a lot happening on the firepower side of it. But the Cyclone Feed System, for example, makes the firepower that is available more reliable. And I see a lot of the other gun makers and even ourselves concentrating on more reliable, more consistent, more efficient equipment.

I also see some room for more reliability in the paintball itself. It seems like that's one area of the industry that hasn't developed a lot. The balls can be damaged by moisture, or humidity, or if it gets too cold. I see some room for improvement and some new materials, maybe a tighter tolerance on the ball so you get more accuracy.

ANDREW: Are you thinking about doing a sidearm at all?

DENNIS: We talk about it once in a while. The big game is becoming more popular. I think the reason for that is that a big game will accommodate any size group: if you've got two guys that want to go play, or if you've got twenty guys who want to go play. And it's more of a fun day rather than a competition where you're working hard all day. You can go out there and you can play as you want and it's pretty relaxing. A fun day.

We do see the need for a sidearm possibly just for that niche of the market, the guys who just play the big games. Big games are not super-strict on the rules, whereas in a tournament you wouldn't necessarily even be allowed to carry a sidearm. I think they're pretty strict on the one gun per player rule there. But the big games, they just want you to have fun. And if you want to take a pistol or something similar out there on the field with you, they're very happy to let you do that.

We also see some demand for a pistol on the law enforcement side for training. And also—this number is debated a little bit—around seventy percent of players play what we call outlaw. Which means they don't play in an organized field setting; they're just a bunch of buddies getting together in the woods somewhere. And we see a demand for the sidearm in that application also.

ANDREW: Sort of like the original days of paintball, going back to the roots, with fewer shots and more hunting.

DENNIS: Yeah, plus the guys that play outlaw paintball make up their own rules. And if they want to carry an extra gun with them and no one else cares, like I said, they make up their own rules, so we definitely see a demand.

FIELDER'S CHOICE

The appendix in the back of this book provides a list of paintball fields in all areas of the United States and of the world, so you've got plenty of options when it comes to locating a field. If you haven't played for a few years, however, you may be in for the surprise of your life when you get there.

Paintball isn't just that game you play in the woods anymore.

The concept fields used for tournaments are now easily obtainable by field owners willing to set aside space to put them up. There are even parks set up in family fun centers next to go-karts and batting cages! This availability is due to many new companies coming into the arena game market. In addition to the Sup'air system, Ultimate Air has begun to make bunkers that are tubeless, so they can be put up in more remote areas without the pipes Sup'air uses.

Jungle of Doom

Courtesy Challenge Park Xtreme

Bedlam, IL

Courtesy Challenge Park Xtreme

Many fields have gone even further than that. Although theme fields are not new— SC Village has been doing them since the 1980s—they are home to a whole new kind of theatrics. Probably the most graphic example is Challenge Park, just outside of Chicago, IL. They were an established field for years, then moved in order to facilitate something bigger: a theme park for paintball. Their fields include, among others:

- **Bedlam, IL.** This field is a town. Full buildings, cars parked in the streets, mailboxes, phone booth, streetlights, the works.

- **Jungle of Doom** is a wooded field with a full temple built into it.

- **Armageddon** is a bombed-out cityscape with rubble piles and half-destroyed buildings.

Armageddon

Courtesy Challenge Park Xtreme

Meanwhile, in Canada, a field opened up in Toronto using the abandoned set from "Total Recall". Now called "Area 51", the field has a backdrop that is, literally, something out of a sci-fi movie.

The concept isn't new. EMR has had the "Castle" for years, and holds two "Castle Conquests" every year. Skirmish has several theme fields, like "Hood in the Woods". But the level of theatrics has become so high that, again, paintball fields resemble theme parks more and more.

But what about the good old woods fields? They're still out there. If you just want to play out in the woods, that's still available. But, given what's being done today, look for theme-park field owners to keep trying to top each other in the years to come. The future of scenario paintball is limited only by what field owners are willing to build—and, for the moment, they show no signs of slowing down.

—*Rob Tyger Rubin*

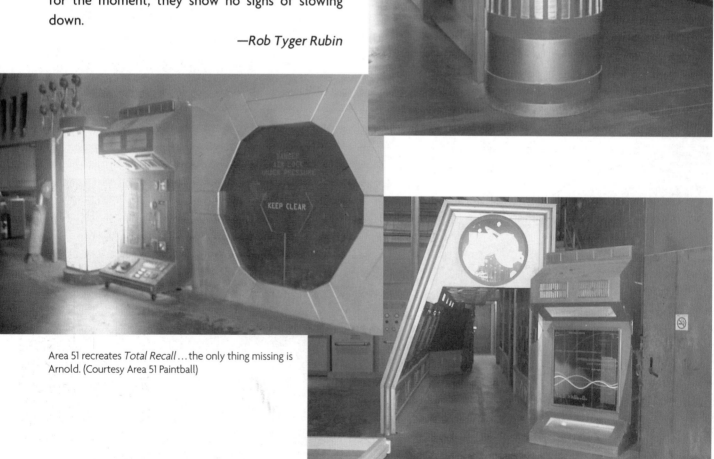

Area 51 recreates *Total Recall* ... the only thing missing is Arnold. (Courtesy Area 51 Paintball)

A WHOLE NEW BREED OF
SCENARIO GAMES

Scenario games have exploded in popularity over the past few years. Scenario games are somewhat different than the big games mentioned in the first edition of this book. They have storylines, as well as characters, plots, and props—more like miniature movies than paintball games. Each player is assigned a character, usually with cards that have abilities or powers, and they're let loose on the field. Teams complete missions for points, and at the end of the game, the team with the most points wins.

There are a few types of players in every game. Most players will be your basic player. Their characters will usually be ground units of some kind, who actually carry out most of the objectives. The minority of players are the "rollers", the role-players. These are the generals, the XO's, the grand pooh-bahs of the game. They achieve mission goals that involve little, if any, actual shooting. Instead, rollers use a lot of talking, diplomacy, and sometimes outright lying in order to carry out their tasks.

One of the big battles at Viper Scenarios' "Texas Revolution VII: The Quest for the Holy Grail" in 2001. The event was held at Paintball USA in Houston. (© James R. Morgan, Sr.)

Whatever level you're on, however, your actions can have a major impact on what happens in the game. If you get a mission that says, "Go get the fuel from the fuel dump and bring it back", your ability (or inability) to do that can affect future missions. You may need the fuel to use a special weapon, or a tank, or any amount of things. The ability to stick to the missions is one of the main factors in determining whether teams win or lose scenario games.

Many people have been playing scenario games in recent years, and, win or lose, they've had fun at it. Right now there are several scenario games that make nation-wide circuits every year, most notably those produced by MXS, Wayne Dollack Scenario Games, and Viper Scenario Series. It used to be that if you wanted to experience a scenario game, you had to go to a home field of the scenario producer. Now, they travel all over the country making scenario games accessible to anyone.

All large scenario games have a few things in common. One is the longer game format. MXS and Dollack both have 24-hour games, meaning they start at noon on Saturday, end at noon Sunday, and are played all through the night. If you get eliminated, you go to a dead zone and jump

The Foletta brothers as Sir Bedemere and his squire at The Quest for the Holy Grail ((c) James R. Morgan, Sr.)

back into the game after a specific time interval, usually about 15 minutes. The action can be as non-stop or as casual as you like.

Scenario games are also becoming available locally. Many small fields now offer scenario-style games to play on special weekends. These games are great for casual players who want to try out scenario play without investing in a hotel room and a lot of gas money. Sometimes, local venues don't provide the quality of game or staffing that you might get from a larger company, but that's your tradeoff: some quality for a local feel.

If you are in the mood for a road trip, however, there are a lot of field-specific scenario games that are worth the car ride. EMR's "Quest" scenario is still a popular game, attracting players from all parts. There are also some scenario games that they can only hold once. Challenge Park is holding a scenario game during the summer of 2002 that features William Shatner as a guest captain. For obvious reasons, it would be hard to do that game more than once.

With more and more players signing up for scenario games, it's never been easier to find one to suit your needs and interests. Get into the game this season, and try one out for yourself!

—Rob Tyger Rubin

CODES AND COMMUNICATION

TALK IT UP

In the sport of paintball and *especially* within the ranks of its top tournaments, good teamwork is the key to success. The execution of good teamwork involves the integration of a number of important factors, the single most important of which is communication. Good communication requires commitment and dedication from all members of a team in order to learn how to effectively spread important information during a game. The history of paintball shows us that it is those groups of players who have developed their ability to function as a *single unit* on the field of play, rather than as five or ten individuals playing individually on the same team, that have been most successful.

An integral part of communication on today's tournament paintball fields involves the widespread use of *codes*. Today's tournament teams go to extreme measures in order to learn how to communicate effectively among themselves without giving away important information to their opponents. A full set of codes for a single team usually involves code words to account for any relevant circumstance that might be encountered on the field of play.

Here is a list of codes as they might be within a serious tournament team. *These are merely examples*, and this list is not necessarily exhaustive of the entire range of items for which teams designate specific codes. Different teams' codes can vary greatly depending upon a number of factors, but dedication to learning them and strict adherence to their use is of utmost importance if a team is to succeed on the tournament paintball field.

Code Word	Code Meaning	Code Application
Burn 1, 2, 3…	# of opponents eliminated	Calling out "Burn 1" signifies that you have eliminated one of your opponents; "Burn 2" = two eliminations; "Burn 3" = three eliminations; and so forth.
Down 1, 2, 3…	# of own teammates eliminated	Calling out "Down 1" signifies that you have eliminated one of your opponents; "Down 2" = two eliminations; "Down 3" = three eliminations; and so forth.
Reality	amount of time left in game	"Reality four-fifty" = four minutes and fifty seconds left in the game; "Reality ten-ten" = ten minutes and ten seconds left in the game; etc.
Thunder	provide cover fire	This is a code you might call out if you were preparing to shift from one bunker to another and needed cover fire in order to make it happen. Variations of and additions to this code could further specify where the cover fire needed to be directed, for example.
Rabbit	wanting to move	Variations on this code could specify your plan of action, and this code could be used in conjunction with codes such as "Thunder."
Poison	marker down	Use this code to inform the rest of your team that your marker is experiencing problems during the game, or has quit working entirely.
Fast Food	need to reload	Use this code to inform nearby teammates that your marker's loader is running low on paint and that you need to reload.
Choker	bunkering code	In tournament paintball, there are times when it is necessary to run up on an opponent and eliminate him or her at point-blank range. This is commonly known as a "bunker move," and the code to direct teammates to do it or to alert teammates that you are about to do it is one of the most important ones to have.
Wolverine	push upfield	This code is sometimes used near the end of a game when there is danger of time running out. When a team calls it out, the entire team will move upfield at once in an attempt to overrun their opponents and win the game.
Shadow	opponent is across the bunker from you	To warn a teammate that he occupies the opposite side of the same bunker as one of his opponents, call out "Shadow" along with his name.

In addition to learning code words for communicating actions and circumstances effectively across a team, the nature of today's concept fields (especially the inflatable fields) has made it possible for teams and players to give specific names to bunkers with characteristic shapes. By giving specific names to these bunkers, teams are better able to communicate positions and locations on the field.

Can: A cylindrical bunker set on its end, standing approximately seven feet tall with a diameter of roughly four feet. "Cans" are most commonly found in the backfield, nearest each team's respective starting stations.

Can

Steamroller: A "can" that has been laid on its side.

Dorito: This bunker resembles a pyramid, is roughly eight feet in height, and is one of the most popular Sup'air bunkers made.

Baby Dorito: Just as it sounds, a smaller version of the "Dorito."

Dorito

Wing Nut: Looks like a "can" which has been cut in half, with two fins that stick out from the sides of the bunker.

Wing Nut

Snake: There's no mistaking this bunker; it looks exactly like the name implies and is typically found across the midfield running near the out-of-bounds line. "Snakes" are low bunkers and the players who have become most comfortable using them are those who have learned how to crawl and snapshoot very well.

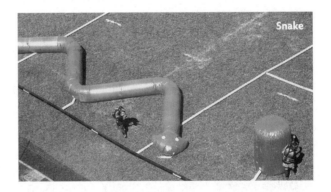

Snake

Nessie: This bunker resembles a miniature snake, very short in length and displaying a characteristic "S"-curve.

Car Wash: An arch that forms a long tunnel when set up on the field—hence the name "car wash." It is typically found along the midfield line and can easily provide cover for two or more players from each team, even at the same time!

Cone: Looks like a pointed ice cream cone (a "sugar cone") which has

Cone

Submarine

Carrot

X

been turned upside down and sits on its circular surface, pointing towards the sky.

Carrot: A "cone" that has been laid on its side.

Submarine: This is a large bunker that will almost always be found on the midfield line next to one of the tapelines (out-of-bounds borders). It roughly resembles the long-tube appearance of a submarine.

Fish: There is no mistaking this bunker when you see it; it looks like a fish.

Rocket: As is the case above, there is no mistaking the "rocket"; it looks exactly as one would expect a "rocket" to look.

Octopus: This bunker is typically found in the exact center of the field, and resembles a large X laid on the ground with a single cone pointing straight up from the center of the X.

Tombstone: Like the snake, rocket, and fish, the "tombstone" looks exactly as its name implies.

X: When laid down and viewed from above, this bunker forms an "X" on the ground.

T: Resembles a "T" on the ground when viewed from above.

Piggie: This is one of the most interesting bunkers in paintball. It is a low-to-the-ground tube that stands on two triangular "legs," one on each end of the tube. The resulting shape is similar to the appearance of a "Weiner dog," but the cosmetic accents of a face on one side of the tube and a curly-Q tail on the other side give it the unmistakable look of a pig.

Taco: This is another no-brainer; it almost perfectly resembles the shape of the typical taco.

—*Justin Owen*

Fish

Cheese: Resembles the shape of a thin, tall, triangular slice of cheese standing on end.

Wedge: Somewhat resembles the "cheese" with its top half cut off.

Piggie

The Complete Guide to Paintball

Courtesy Adrenaline Games

HANDY HAND SIGNALS

Visual signals are used when it's time to be stealthy and quiet. You and your buddy may be crawling to the flag station unnoticed. Why give away your position by talking? Using visual hand signals, you can communicate to each other silently as you plan your attack.

The following hand signals have been adopted from Navy SEAL small unit tactical signals. Of course they've been slightly modified to meet the challenges of the paintball experience.

Stop
Fist held in air.

Hear
Hold your hand up next to your ear as if you are listening.

Go
Arm up, sweeps from back to front.

Down
Arm forward, sweeps down.

Cover Me
Tap your head with your hand.

See
Point to your eyes.

Go Faster
Fist in air, pumps up and down rapidly.

Out of Air
Fast movement of the hand back
and forth across the throat.

Gun Down
Point "thumbs down" at your gun.

BOTTOM LINE

A style of constant air system where the ASA adapter is located at the bottom of the paintball gun's grip frame. This ASA adapter is where the constant air tank is connected to the paintgun. The ASA adapter may be designed into the grip frame so as to be part of the grip frame or it may be a after market ASA adapter that is mounted to the bottom of the grip frame. If it is a after market ASA adapter it will have to have a gas line connecting it to the paintgun in order to allow gas to flow from the tank into and through the ASA adapter to the gas line and then to the paintgun.

BREECH DROP LOADING

Guns using breech loading systems load into an area larger than the inner diameter of the barrel. The ball must then be up into the barrel.

BREECH LOCK SYSTEM

A design that prevents the paintgun from being accidentally pumped twice before it is fired once. Breech locking guns must be fired before the gun can be pumped again.

BUTT PLATE

A device that fits on to the end of a tank allowing it to be used as a shoulder stock.

CALIBER

With respect to a paintball the diameter of a circular section. With reference to a paintgun the diameter of the bore of a gun taken as a unit of measurement.

CALIFORNIA STYLE

A style of constant air system developed in California in the late 1980's that consisted of a paintgun, a 'L' shape shoulder stock with a constant air tank holder located on the bottom side of it, a constant air tank of either 7 or 10 ounce in size with a Thermo on/off valve that would be held in the shoulder stock's tank holder and a hose with fittings that would connect the tank to the paintgun.

CARBON DIOXIDE

Also known as CO_2. A colorless, odorless, incombustible gas that has many purposes such as dry ice, the carbonation in carbonated beverages, and in fire extinguishers. CO_2 is present in the atmosphere and formed during respiration. CO_2 is a compound gas made of oxygen and carbon. CO_2 stores it's energy when it is in a liquid state and releases it into a usable force through expansion into a gas. Used in paintguns as a pressurized gas (power source) for shooting paintballs out of the paintgun's barrel. With respect to semi auto paintguns, CO_2 is also used for recocking the paintgun.

CGA

Denotes Compressed Gas Association. Usually used to refer to a cylinder valve outlet connection detailed in the CGA pamphlet V-1.

CHECK VALVE

Allows substance (such as gas, liquid or solids) to flow in only one direction. Once passed the check valve the substance cannot flow back through check valve.

CHRONOGRAPH

Electronic device that measures the speed of an object directed across it.

CO_2

The abbreviation for Carbon Dioxide.

CONSTANT AIR

A terminology developed in California in the late 1980's. It refers to the use of a refillable gas tank that is connected to a paintgun and supplies the CO_2 gas necessary to power the operation of the gun. The term "Constant Air" was derived from the fact that the paintgun would have a prolonged supply of gas and would be able to get 300–1000 shots per tank of gas, depending on size of tank and type of gun. This was opposed to paintguns that used 12 gram CO_2 cartridges and only got 15–25 shots per cartridge on the average.

CRITICAL TEMPERATURE

The temperature above which liquid phase cannot exist.

CRITICAL PRESSURE

The saturation vapor pressure at the Critical Temperature.

CYCLE RATE

Indicates the number of cycles a paintgun can perform per second.

DETENT, BALL

Sometimes call Ball stop, anti-doubler, wire nubbin. A device that keeps no more than one paintball from loading into the chamber of a paintgun when the paintgun is executing one cycle. It does this by maintaining the paintball in a stationary position until the paintguns bolt pushes the paintball into the barrel of the gun.

DEW POINT

The temperature and pressure at which the liquefaction of a vapor begins.

DIRECT FEED

A system by which paintballs are fed directly into the paintgun chamber or barrel via a feed nipple. The feed nipple is usually fastened to side of the paintgun at a 45 degree angle. Feed nipples on pump action guns are usually 1" in diameter and feed nipples on semi auto paintguns are usually 7/8" in diameter.

DISK, RUPTURE

A small copper disk in the valve of a tank that is designed to rupture if the pressure in the tank becomes too great. The rupture disk is usually held in place by a safety plug that has vent holes in it.

DONKEY

Slang for ASA Adapter.

DOT

Abbreviation for Department of Transportation whose Title 49, Code of Federal Regulations regulate the movement of hazardous materials.

DOUBLE ACTION

Requiring only one pull of the trigger to cock and fire.

ELBOW

Slang for hopper adapter.

EXPANSION CHAMBER

A device which conditions CO_2 gas by allowing it to expand before it enters the paintgun's valve system.

FEED NIPPLE

Also known as Feed port. The feed nipple is a short tube that is connected to the paintgun housing at an angle of 45 degrees. It provides the passage by which paintballs move from the paintball hopper, through the hopper adapter, which attaches to the feed nipple, and into the chamber of the paintgun. Commonly, feed nipples for pump action paintguns are one inch in diameter, while semi auto paintguns have seven eighths inch feed nipples.

FEED PLUG

A plug at the bottom of a power feeder that angles the balls into the feed port. It can also be turned to stop the balls from feeding into your gun.

FEED TUBE

A paintball storage container tubular in form, closed at one end and open at other end with some type of lid covering the opening. When playing paintball the player uses the feed tube to reload his paintgun's hopper.

FEEDER

Slang for hopper.

FILL STATION

An apparatus consisting of at least one valve used for exhausting pressurized fill hose, a fill hose and some type of fill adapter for connecting a constant air tank to one end of the hose. It is used for filling smaller constant air tanks with liquid Co_2 from larger siphon fill tank. The large siphon fill tank is usually 50 to 60 pounds in volume weight.

FITTING, ELBOW, (90 DEGREE)

A fitting that allows the connection of two items at a 90 degree angle to each other. Such as a CA hose to make a ASA adapter or paintgun.

FLAG STATION

With reference to the game of paintball, this is a team's base camp and is the location where a team's flag is kept. It is also the location where a team must return the opposing team's flag in order to win the game.

FLANK

1. The extreme right or left side of an army or fleet.

2. To stand or be placed or posted at the flank or side of.

3. To defend or guard at the flank.

4. To menace or attack the flank of.

FOGGING UP

This refers to those times when a person's breathing and lack of movement will cause the lenses of a persons goggles to fog over, severely reducing visibility.

FORE GRIP

A horizontal grip generally located on the front of a gun. This grip is generally grasped with the players off hand; i.e. the hand not on the trigger frame; to stabilize the gun for shooting.

F.P.S.

Abbreviation for 'feet per second'. This is the standard method in the U.S. for determining the speed at which a paintgun is shooting.

GAS EFFICIENCY

Refers to the amount of shots a gun gets in relation to the amount of liquid Co2 it uses. Similar to miles per gallon; i.e. getting 350 shots from a seven ounce constant air tank.

GOGGLES

Eye protection worn by players to prevent eye damage. Paintball goggles are specifically designed for the sport of paintball and should not be substituted with goggles made for any other application other than paintball.

GOING LIQUID

Refers to liquid Co_2 entering the paintgun before it has had a chance to expand into a gas or vapor.

GRIPS

Components that fit on the paintgun grip frame and provide surface area by which the shooter may grip the gun. Grips are replaceable on many types of paintguns. Different styles of grips can provide greater comfort and ease of use for the individual paintball player. Different styles of grips include rubber, wood, and wraparound types.

HAMMER

Also known as The lower bolt or the striker. This component, when released from the cocked position, strikes the valve assembly and forces it open. When this striking of the valve assembly by the hammer occurs, CO_2 is allowed to pass through the valve assembly from the gas source to the paintgun barrel.

HAMMER (DOWN)

Refers to pulling the trigger, putting paint on someone is a sudden and intense manner, seizing the moment on offense by showering a target with paint.

HAMMER SEAR

The part of a gun that retains the hammer in a fixed position, usually under main spring pressure. When the trigger is pulled by the shooter's finger, it pushes against the sear allowing it to release the hammer and thus allowing the hammer to strike the valve assembly.

HARNESS

The combination of straps, pouches and other parts forming the working gear worn by a paintball player to carry paintball, CO_2 cartridges, tanks, squeegee and anything else he/she requires to play the game of paintball.

HOSE

In paintball a hose is used to transfer gas from one component to another. Such as from a constant air tank to a ASA adapter on a paintgun.

HONE

A tool that is mechanically rotated and has abrasive tip(s) for polishing or enlarging holes to precise dimensions.

HOPPER

A container used to hold paintballs, usually with a lid that covers the opening where the paintballs are loaded into it, and has a feed nipple at it's bottom.

HOSING

Refers to consistent rapid firing. A tactic typically used when pinning down an opposing player.

HYDROSTATIC TEST

A container test required at definite intervals by DOT to determine the wall thickness via measuring elastic expansion. Purpose of the test is to assure the container is safe for continued use.

I.D.

Abbreviation for inner diameter.

IN-LINE CONFIGURATION

Refers to the manner in which the bolt and hammer of a paintgun are positioned in relation to each other. An in-line configuration indicates that the bolt and hammer are in line with each other one behind the other.

LENSES, THERMAL

A dual lens system. The outer lens is made of a super hard polycarbonate material. The inner lens is made of a different polycarbonate composition that allows anti fog jell coat to stick to it. The two lenses are attached to each other by means of a rubber gasket that makes an air tight seal between the two. The space between the two lenses is called a thermal barrier and helps to reduce fogging on the inner lens.

LOADER

Slang for hopper feed tube.

LIQUID

Slang for CO_2 in liquid form.

Where to Find the Game You Love

A state by state and international listing of fields, manufacturers, distributors and shops involved in the paintball industry

U.S.A. PLAYING FIELDS & SHOPS

ALABAMA

Advanced AL Adventures
7880 Bear Creek Rd.
Sterrett, AL 35243
205 672-2860

Paintball Pro Shop
7880 Bear Creek Rd.
Sterrett, AL 35243
205 967-8661

Splat Alley
705 McKinley Ave
Huntsville, AL 35801
205-539-5959

ARIZONA

The Command Post
1432 N Scottsdale Rd.
Tempe, AZ 85281
602-970-6329

The Command Post
4139 West Bell Rd. Ste 2
Phoenix, AZ 85023
602 863-2569

Desert Fox Paintball 9651 S. Houghton
Tuscon, AZ 85747
520-574-9232

The Paintball Store, Inc.
1601 E. Bell Rd. #A5
Phoenix, AZ 85022
602-923-7585,
923-7544 fax

Survival & Army Surplus
15231 N Cave Creek Rd
Phoenix, AZ 85032
602-482-6663

Westworld Paintball
2920 W. Thomas Rd.
Phoenix, AZ 85017
602-447-8200

ARKANSAS

First Assault
Route 51
Arkadelphia, AR 71923
501-245-3549

Paintball Arkansas
Mayflower, AR 72106
501-470-4400

CALIFORNIA

ABC Paintball
535 Salmar Ave., Unit B
Campbell, CA 95008
408-866-9222

Action Paintball
240 North Broadway
Escondido, CA 92025
760-738-1097

Adventure Game
3604 Ross Avenue
San Jose, CA 95124
408-723-1455

Adventure Game Supp
17618 Sherman Way
Van Nuys, CA 91405
818-708-3384

American Canyon Pball
Jungle, Vallejo, CA
www.paintballjungle.com
707-552-2426

Auction Surplus
512 South Blosser Rd
Santa Maria, CA 93454
805-928-7408

B&M Paintball
605 No. Azusa Ave.
Azusa, CA 91702
(818) 334-0498

Bear Creek Pursuit Pball
584 Cestaric Dr.
Milpitas, CA 95035
408-946-7676

Bud Orr's Pro Shop
13517 Alondra Blvd.
Santa Fe Springs, CA
90670
310-407-2898

Cambrian Surplus
2059 Woodard Rd.
San Jose, CA 95124
408-377-6953

Central Coast Pball Park
4765 Santa Margarita Lk
Santa Margarita, CA
93453
805-481-1476

Central Coast Pball Park
1554 West Beach Street
Arroyo Grande, CA 93420
805-481-1476

Check Yourself Paintball
5708C Hollister Ave.
Goleta, CA 93117
805-967-6190

Delta Archery's Splat Div
1820-D Arnold Ind. Way
Concord, CA 94520
510-685-7141

Eagles's Nest
PO Box 1788
Valley Center, CA 92082
619-749-0281

Gramps & Grizzly
7203 Arlington Ave.,
Riverside, CA 92503
909-359-4859

Gramps & Grizzly
2085 River Rd. #B
Norco, CA 91760
909-278-0173

Hobby World
18575 Valley Blvd.
Bloomington, CA 92316
714-824-1747

Indoor Speedball
15000 Avalon
Gardena, CA 90248
213-323-1021

I & I Sports Co., Inc.
1524 W. 178th St.
Gardena, CA 90248
310-715-6800

I & I Sports Co., Inc.
15349 A Los Gatos Blvd.
Los Gatos, CA 95032
408-358-9774, 358-9864

I & I Sports Co., Inc.
18232 E. Gale Ave.
Industry, CA 91748
626-810-5523

I & I Sports Co., Inc.
2957 S Sepulveda Blvd.
Los Angeles, CA 90064
310-444-9988

I & I Sports Co., Inc.
19751 S Fugueroa St.
Carson, CA 90745

I & I Sports Co., Inc.
5637 Cottle Rd.
San Jose, CA 95123
408-224-6800

J&S Surplus
Highway 1 & Struve Rd.
Moss Landing, CA 95039
408-724-0588

Jungle Island Pball Pk
Lake Elsinore, CA
Lake St. @ 15 FWY
1-800-5 JUNGLE

Jungle Supply
2840 E. College
Visalia, CA 93292
209-636-3128

KAPP Paintball
65 Brockwood Ave.
Santa Rosa, CA 95405
707-571-1077

KAPP Paintball
57 w. Barham Ave.
Santa Rosa, CA 95407
707-571-8068;571-81497

Kingsmen Shop
201 North Hill St.
Oceanside, CA 92054
619-722-5108

Maximum Pball Supp.
4741 N. Blackstone Ave.
Fresno, CA 93726
559-222-3814

North County Paintball
San Marcos, CA 92069
619-440-5944; 273-4444

Outdoor World
1440 41st Ave.
Capitola, CA 95010
408-479-1501

Outdoor World
3903 Santa Rita Road
Pleasanton, CA 94566
510-463-3221

Outdoor World
222 No. Freemont St.
Montery, CA 93940
408-373-3615

Pacific Paintball Supply
3181 ClevelandAve. #C
Santa Rosa, CA 95403
707-571-1077

Paintball Paradise
260 Shotwell Street
San Francisco, CA 94110
415-552-5335

Palmer's Pursuit Shop
3951 Development Dr
Unit #3
Sacramento, CA 95838
916-923-9676

SC Village
River Road & Hellman St.
Corona, CA 91720
949-489-9000

Skan-Line Game Supp
1677 Superior Ave, Unit H
Costa Mesa. CA 92627
714-645-LINE

Skirmish. Inc.
7361 Reseda
Reseda. CA 91335
818-705-6322

Spotcha Paintball
828 N. 2nd St.
El Cajon. CA 92021

Strategic Game Supply
10680 Katella Ave.
Anaheim, CA 92804
714-772-6422

Surplus City
4106 Franklin Blvd.
Sacramento, CA 95820
916-485-1120

Survival Sports
4800 Minnesota Ave.
Fair Oaks, CA 95628
916-965-1770

Tagline
9077 Arrow Route 100
Cucamonga, CA 91730
909-481-7753, 481-7754 fax

T.A.S.O.
15950 Downey Ave.
Paramount, CA 90723
310-531-0515

Unique Sporting
10680 Katella Ave.
Anaheim, CA 92804
714-772-6422

Velocity Paintball
4248 B Bonita Road
Bonita, CA 91902
619-470-3533

Velocity Paintball
12623 Poway Rd.
Poway, CA 92064
619-513-2778

Warped Sportz
11919 W. Pico Blvd.
Los Angeles, CA 90064
310-914-9222,
914-9511 fax

COLORADO

Adventure Game
425 Thames Dr.
Colo. Springs, CO 80906
303-893-4263

Dragon Man's Pball Pk
1225 Dragon Man Dr.
Colo. Springs CO 80929
719-683-2200

Pro-Star Sports
PO Box 1280
Littleton, CO 80160
303-972-4113

Rocky Mountain Pball
430 W. Fillmore
Co. Springs, CO 80907
719-473-3725; 473-3576 fax

Rocky Mountain Pball
7500 So. University #110
Littleton, CO 80122
303-689-7608

RMT Sports
PO Box 1280
Littleton, CO 80160
303-972-4113

Warped Sportz
3970 S. Broadway
Englewood, CO 80110
303-806-9721

Finding Paintball

CONNECTICUT

The Gun Rack
240A Rt. 21,
Cnty. Home Rd.
Thompson, CT 06277
203-928-151

Hogan's Alley Paintball
445 State Street
North Haven, CT 06473
203-288-2746

Hogan's Alley Paintball
998 No. Colony Rd.
Meriden, CT 06450
203-238-2875

Paintball Plus
5 Padanaram Rd.
Danbury, CT 06811
203-730-8850

Splattown, USA
223 Merrow Rd. Rt. 195
Tolland, CT 06084
860-870-9737

DELAWARE

Paintball Adventures LLC
1438 Woodmill Dr.
Dover, DE 19904
302-736-5777

FLORIDA

Elite Forces Field
Cowcreek Road
Edgewater, FL
904-767-2131

Extreme Rage Al Sports
3598 Fowler St.
Ft. Myers, FL 33901
941-939-0911, 939-5141 fx

Florida Paintball Center
8440 Ulmerton, #500
Largo, FL 34641
813-538-9946

GI Jeff's
5257 S Ridgewood Ave
Allandale, FL 32123
904-767-2131

G&H Sterling LTD
8362 Pines Blvd., #290
Pembroke Pines, 33024
305-438-7571

Guerrilla Games
111 W. Olympia Ave.
Punta Gorda, FL 33950
813-627-8865

Hi-Tec Paintball Park
PO Box 301
Bradenton, FL 34206
941-746-5866

Holly Army Navy
3440 Ave. G, N.W.
Winter Haven, FL 33880
813-967-5920

Paintball Experts
70 W. 49th St.
Hialeah, FL 33012
305-823-6892

Paintball Park
8240 Durrance Rd.
Ft. Myers, FL
941-939-0911, 598-1015

Pursuit Paintball Games
5132 Conroy Rd., #918
Orlando, FL 32811
407-843-3456

Paintball World
3445 Vineland Road
Orlando, FL 32811
407-648-8404

South Florida Paintball
7232 S.W. 8th St. Ste 2
Miami, FL 33144
305-267-1122

South Florida Indoor Paintball
2801 SW 31st Ave.
Pembroke Park, FL 33009
954-893-8284

Space Coast
3600 Garden Street
Titusville, FL 32796
321-264-4484

Splat Attack
10129 SW 72nd St.
Miami, FL 33173
305-412-9991

Splat Inc.
2418 No. Monroe St.
Tallahassee, FL 32303
850-385-4467

Sunny's at Sunset
Sunrise, FL 33322
305-741-2070

Survival City
111 W. Olympia Ave.
Punta Gorda, FL 33950
813-639-1100

Tropic Trades
9696 S.W. 40th St.
Miami, FL 33165
305-221-1371

Warped Sportz
2294-12 Mayport Rd.
Jacksonville, FL 32233
904-242-0012

Wayne's World of Pball
4841 S. Pine St.
Ocala, FL 34480
352-401-1801

Xtreme Paintball
3561 NW 9th Ave.
Oakland Park, FL 33309
305-564-5451

GEORGIA

A-1 Pball Forest & Supply
W. Pine Chapel Rd.
Calhoun, GA 30701
706-625-0072

Appalachian Paintball
1116 So. Thornton Ave.
Dalton, GA 30720
706-226-1765

Bay's Paintball
501 Eve Street
Augusta, GA 30904
706-733-1055

Georgia Paintball
1289 Roswell Rd.
Marrietta, GA 3062
770-971-8040

Indoor Paint Games
285A Lake Mirror Road
Forest Park, GA 30050
404-361-6740

Insane Paintball
986 Battlefield Pkwy.
Ft. Oglethorpe, GA 30742
706-866-2121

Mountain Adventure Games
123 So. Campus Rd.
Lookout Mtn., GA 30750
706-820-4419

Outer Limits
220 Holbrook Drive SW
Rome, GA 30165
706-234-9896

Splat Zone Indoor
5050 Jimmy Carter Blvd.
Norcross, GA 30093
404-441-9333

Wildfire Paintball
1989 Tucker Ind. Rd.
Tucker, GA 30084
770-493-8978

Wildfire Paintball
7301 Campbellton Rd.
Atlanta, GA 30331
770-493-8978

Wildfire Paintball
2641 Hesterton Rd.
Madison, GA
770-493-8978

Wildfire Paintball
2191 Rabbit Hill Cr.
Dacula, GA 30211
770-493-8978

HAWAII

Xlent Services
PO Box 2271
Ewa Beach, HI 96706
808-671-1110

IDAHO

Winders
5515 E Iona Rd
Iona, ID 83427
208-523-2475

Walter Middy's MMOV
6759 Supply Way
Boise, ID 83705
208-429-1276

IOWA

ICU Paintball Worgamz Inc.
4489 NW 2nd Ave..
Des Moines, IA 50313
515-282-9080

North Iowa Arms
810 North 8th Street
Clear Lake, IA 50428
515-357-3545

Total Paintball
324 E. 4th St.
Davenport, IA 52801
319-324-0276
322-4262 fax

ILLINOIS

Air America
2275 S. Mt. Prospect Rd.
Des Plaines, IL 60018
847-545-9999

Bad Boyz Toyz
888 So. Rt. 59, #104
Naperville, IL 60565
630-355-8808

Bad Boyz Toyz
17913 Torrence Ave.
Lansing, IL 60438
708-418-8888

Bad Boyz Toyz
15160 LaGrange Rd.
Orland Park, IL 60462
708-460-1122

Bad Boyz Toyz Skokie
7135 Central Ave.
Skokie, IL 60077
847-679-9125

Bad Boyz Toyz
700 N Milwaukee, #133.
Vernon Hills, IL 60061
847-362-4848

Challenge Games-Aurora
2256 Fox Valley Ctr D21A
Aurora, IL 60504
630-499-1025
499-1045 fax

Fox River Pball Sports
1891 N Farnsworth
Aurora, IL 60505
630-585-5651

Operation Paintball
15N850 Brier Hill Rd..
Hampshire, IL 60140
630-736-9107

Pursuit Adventure
956 S. Bartlett Rd, # 282
Bartlett, IL 60103
630-736-9107, 736-9132

Rockford Pball
7821 No. 2nd St.
Macheseney Park, 61115
815-282-2992

Strange Ordnance
914 Greenwood Ave.
Glenview, IL 60025
708-998-8312

Video Smideo
10408 Rte. 47
Huntley, IL 60142
847-669-3225

Wyld Side Sports Inc.
8750 N. Second St..
Machesney Park, IL 61115
815-636-9970

INDIANA

Adventure Zone
8641 East 116th St.
Fishers, IN 46038

Blast Camp
608 Third Street
Hobart, IN 46342
219-947-7733

Blast Camp
109 9th St.
Michigan City, IN 46360
219-947-7733

Dark Armies
2525 N Shadelands Ave.
Indianapolis, IN 46219
317-353-1987

Fantasy Fields Paintball
PO Box 194
Denver, IN 46926
765-985-3068

Gator Joe's Pball Supp
1223 S. Girls School Rd.
Indianapolis, IN 46231
317-247-0410

Indianapolis Army & Navy
6032 East 21st
Indianapolis, IN 46219
317-356-0858

Indy Extreme
9508 Haver Way
Indianapolis, IN 46240
317-566-9115

Michiana Paintball Club
In&Outdoor Fields, Store
Scottsdale Mall, S Bend
219-291-2540

Paint Ball Sports
7800 S. Anthony Blvd.
Ft. Wayne, IN 46816
219-447-3379

Warped Sportz
1515 W 81st Ave.
Merrillville, IN 46410
219-736-6111

IOWA

Velocity Paintball
1324 5th Street
Coralville, IA 52241
319-351-4245

KANSAS

Drop Zone Extreme Sports
403 B So. Parker
Olathe, KS 66062
913-768-0200
785-841-1884

Victory Paintball
95th & Renner Blvd.
Lenexa, KS 66212
913-397-0966

KENTUCKY

American Pball Games
8471 US 42, Box #6
Florence, KY 41042
888-440-1088

Xtreme Paintball Sports
3081 Dryden Rd.
Moraine, OH 45439
937-298-5138

OKLAHOMA

Adrenaline Paintball Supp
1280 Interstate Dr.
Norman, OK 73972
405-579-3500

Boot Hill Pball Field
1m. N 1/2m. E Fairgrounds
Stillwater, OK
405-669-2723

Cedar Ridge Pball Games
306 N. 1st
Henryetta, OK 74437
918-652-8891

Dodge City Pball Field
9601 NE 63rd St.
Oklahoma City, OK
405-771-5229

Paintball of Tulsa
6390-H East 31st St.
Tulsa, OK 74135
918-665-7856

Shaggy Bros. Paintball
5575 NW Expressway
Oklahoma City, OK 73114
800-320-7277

SportPaint Inc.
5014 S. Quincy Ave.
Tulsa, OK 74105
918-744-4488

OREGON

Adrenaline—Sportz
9921 SE Stark
Portland, OR 97216
503-251-0065
251-0068 fax

Paintball Games
1820 W. 7th Ave.
Eugene, OR 97402
541-465-4766; fax 4776

Splat Paintball Sports
2880 Ferry SW
Albany, OR 97321
541-928-0957

Warpaint Pball Supply
2304 E. Adams Ave.
Lagrande, OR 97850
503-963-6947

Whack'm & Splak'm
PO Box 58
Keno, OR 97627
503-884-8942

PENNSYLVANIA

Boyd's Front Line
420 Butler Mall
Butler, PA 16001
724-285-8740

E.M.R. Paintball Park
PO Box 728, Rt. 706 & 601
New Milford, PA 18834
570-465-9622

Kuba's Surplus Sales
231 W. 7th St.
Allentown, PA 18102
215-433-3877

Sgt. York's
900 Market St.
Lemoyne, PA 17043
717-761-3819

Wanna-Play Pball Supp
725 North Rte. 15
Dillsburg, PA 17019
717-432-7997

RHODE ISLAND

Boston Pball Supp North
1428 Hartford Ave.
Johnston, RI 02919
401-351-2255

Paintball Wizards of NE
682 Broadway
Pawtucket, RI 02860
401-724-3751

SOUTH CAROLINA

Adrenaline Heaven Pball
1310 Whiskey Rd.
Aiken, S.C. 29801
803-643-8199

Paintball Inc.
155 Verdin Rd.
Greenville, SC 29607
803-458-7221

Paintball Charleston
178 Irby Dr.
Summerville, SC 29483
843-819-7070

The Paintball Store
5131 Dorcester #14
N Charleston, SC 29418
843-552-1115

Pro Fox Paintball
1200 Woodruff Road,
Greenville, SC 29607
803-458-7221

SOUTH DAKOTA

Big Jim's Feud Ranch
HRC30, Box 17
Spearfish, SD 57783
605-578-1808

TENNESSEE

Adventures In Paintball
5600 Brainerd Rd. C-18
Chattanooga, TN 37411
423-485-9077

Challenge Park-Memphis
1345 N. Germantown Pkwy.
Cordova, TN 38018
901-754-4205

The Paintball Store
1345 N. Germantown Pkwy.
Cordova, TN 38018
901-754-4205

TEXAS

Adventure Expeditions
1308 Chestnut St.
Commerce, TX 75248
903-886-7691, 886-3014

Awful Ventures Paintball & More
4309 West Pipeline
Euless, TX 76040
817-282-3636

C.M.Support/ ViewLoader
4921 Olson Drive
Dallas, TX 75227
214-381-3075; 388-6743

Centrex Paintball
Route 7, Box 192
Killeen, TX 76542
817-628-7076

Command Post
8635 Long Point
Houston, TX 77055
713-827-7301

Command Post
10607 I-10 East
Houston, TX 77029
713-675-3221

Command Post
2843 SE Beltway 8
Pasadena, TX 77503
281-998-3233

Constant Action
1701 W Ben White #120
Austin Texas 78704
512-326-1109
326-4072 fax

Constant Action
1319 Rutland
Austin Texas 78758
512-837-3787, 837-4274fx

D.A.M. Games of E Texas
PO Box 5270
Longview, TX 75608
214-297-2075

Green Beret
2213 North 10th St.
McAllen, TX 78051
210-687-1147, 1148

Hit & Run Pball Park
Rt. 2, Box 156D
Mansfield, TX 76063
817-453-8914

Lone Star Paintball
23214 Baneberry
Magnolia, TX 77355
713-356-2158

**Olympic Paintball
Sports**
712 N. 31st
Temple, TX 76504
254-791-5050, 5051 fax

**Olympic Paintball
Sports**
3601 Parmer Lane
Austin, TX 78727
512-834-9290, 834-1934

**Olympic Paintball
Sports**
15010 Fagerquist Rd.
Del Valle, TX 78617

**Olympic Paintball
Sports**
36 White Flint Park Rd.
Temple, TX 76510

Outpost Paintball Field
2341 Murdine Rd.
Aransas Pass, TX 78336
512-758-2181

Paintball Bonanza
S. Main at Chimney Rock
Houston, TX 77035
713-935-0552

**Paintball Games of
Dallas**
3305 E J Carpenter Frwy
Irving, TX 75062
214-554-1937

Pball Game Supp of TX
1101 Royal Pkwy, #117
Euless, TX 76040
817-571-1177

Paintball Gear
7979 N. Eldridge #3018
Houston, TX 77041
281-897-8678

Paintball Gear
12121 NW Freeway
Houston, TX 77092
713-935-0552

Paintball Maxx
5829 W Sam Houston
Pkwy
North, Suite #601
Houston, TX 77041
713-983-9190, 849-3232 fx

Paintball of Waxahachie
507 No. Hwy 77 #614
Waxahachie, TX 75165
972-937-2468

Paintball Player's Supp
7024 Jacksboro Hwy.
Fort Worth, TX 76135
817-237-0299

Paintball Store
9220 FM 1960 West
Houston, TX 77070
201-469-9777

Pball Supp of Lewisville
1081 W. Main St., #107B
Lewisville, TX 75067
972-221-9036

**Survival Games of
Dal/Ft.W**
105 Waits Circle
Garland, TX 75043
817-267-3048

Survival Game of TX
2309 Aldine Meadows
Houston, TX 77032
713-370-GAME

Unicam
2624 Elm Street
Dallas, TX 75226
214-651-1350

West Texas Paintball
2235 19th
Lubbock, TX 79401
806-744-4000

Wolfe City War Games
Rt. 2, Box 267
Wolfe City, TX 75496
903-450-1006

UTAH

CCS 1Air Assault
175 East 400 St #1000
Salt Lake City, UT 84111
801-350-9102

Straight Shooter Pball
3940 Washington Blvd.
Ogden, UT 84403
801-394-2916

VERMONT

3 Guys Games & Pball
1236 Route 4 East
Rutland, VT 05701
802-775-1548

First Downhill
W. Dover, VT 05356
802-464-7743

Mike's Hobbies
162 N. Main Stret
Rutland, VT 05701
802-775-0059

VIRGINIA

B.C.B.G. Paintball
11501 Washington Hwy.
Ashland, VA 23005
804-798-1551

B.C.B.G. Paintball
7540 West Broad St.
Richmond, VA 23294
804-755-4388

Hobby Town of VA
1218 Blue Ridge Ave.
Culpeper, VA 22701
703-825-8729

Pev's Paintball Pro Shop
11204 Lee Highway A-1
Fairfax, VA 22030
703-273-7732, 273-1807 fax

**Pev's Pball Pro
Shop/Games**
13932 Jeff. Davis Hwy.
Woodbridge, VA 22191
703-491-6505

**Pev's Pball Pro
Shop/Games**
2594 Hanco Center Dr.
Woodbridge, VA 22191
703-897-0989

Pev's Paintball Pro Shop
50-A Pidgeon Hill Drive
Sterling, VA 20165
703-709-7387

Pev's Pball Pro Shop
556 Garrisonville Rd.
Stafford, VA 22554
540-720-1319

Splathouse Inc.
946 Grady Ave., Ste. 8
Charlottesville, VA 22901
804-977-5287

WASHINGTON

A.M.S.
18144 Woodinville
Snohomish Rd.
Woodinville, WA 98072
425-483-8855

AWOL Sporting Supply
PO Box 55398
Seattle, WA 98155

AWOL/Splat Mountain
7018 NE Bothell Way
Bothell, WA 98011
206-487-9158

Boomers Paintball
3807 East Sanson
Spokane, WA 99207
509-483-1879

The Jolly Soldier
902A N.E. 65th St.
Seattle. WA 98115
208-524-2266

Mobile Tactics Pball
1829 Hwy. 20 Unit E
Burlington, WA 98233
360-755-9020

Paintball Products NW
205 S. 4th Ave.
Yakima, WA 98902
509-453-4963

Semper Fi Paintball Supp
5373 Guide Meridian #E-3
Bellingham, WA 98226
360-398-8081

Shadow Lake Paintball
22237 196th Ave SE
Renton, WA 98058
206-852-7105

West-Side Pball Supply
6325 Evergreen Way #3
Everett, WA 98203
425-513-6211

West-Side Pball Field
17305 Old Mill Rd.
Snohomish, WA 98290
425-513-6211

Western Paintball
419 B. W. Entiat Ave.
Kennewick, WA 99336
509-585-8353,585-9695

WISCONSIN

Casanova's Outdoor Adventure Store
13735 W. Capitol Drive
Brookfield, WI 53005
262-783-6456;
783-6065 fx

JD Paintball Supplies
7045 Hwy. 70 East
St. Germain, WI 54558
715-479-5838

Paintball Dave's
203 North Broadway
Milwaukee, WI 53202
414-271-3004

Paintball Sam's
Highway K
Racine, WI 53185
414-534-3197

WORLD WIDE WEB

AAA Paintball Park
www.aaapaintballpark.com
Charlie@aaapaintball-park.com

CARIBBEAN

Caribbean Water Craft
1747 Central Ave.
Rio Piedras, PR 00920
809-793-8345

Hunters Paintball Field
O' St. #129 Ramey Base
Aguadilla, PR 00604
787-890-2064

Kings Jewelers
Munoz Riviera, #105
Fajardo. PR 00648
809-863-0909

Seven Seas Bike Shop
53 Union
Fajardo, PR 09648
809-863-8981

TBT Inc.
POBox 1557
Luquillo, PR 00673
809-889-3685

INTERNATIONAL PLAYING FIELDS

UK

ENGLAND

Activ 8 Paintball
62-63 Worcester St.
Wolver Hampton West
Midlands WV2 4LQ, 1901
835444, 1902 835442

Adventure Sports Ltd.
Wedgenock Rifle Range
Wedgenock Lane, War-
nick
Warwickshire, CV35 7PX
01926-491-948

Ashcombe Valley Centre
Ashcombe, Dawlish,
Devon EX7 0QD, 01626-
866766

Belsales
60 Peabody Rd., N. Camp
Farnborough, Hants,,
GU14 6HA; 01252-376827

Bridgehouse Survival
51 Caldervale Ave.,
Charlton-Cum-Hardy,
Manchester, M21 7PN,
0161-445-8804

CCS Leisure
20 Griffith St, Rushden,
Northampton, NN10 0RL
01933-314805

Cheltenham Paintball
Unit 3, The Vineyards
Glouchester Rd,
Cheltenham
Glouchestershire
01242-245504

Global Leisure
95a Nutwick Road
Havant, Hampshire,
PO9 2UQ
01705-499-494

Grizzley Sports
11 St. Margarets Crescent
Putney, London,
SW15 6HL
0181-780-0480

Hook Gun Company
399 Hook Rd.,
Chessington
Surrey, KT9 1EL

Lodge Bushes Pball
49 Salisbury Grove
Giffard Park,
Milton Keynes
B'hamshire, MK14 5QA
01908-618-386

L.S.E.
20 Mt. Vernon Rd,
Barnsley,
S. Yorkshire, S70 4DJ

London Paintball Co.
3 Kirkdale Close
Chatham, Kent, DA1 5BH
01634-864-173

Marksmann Paintball
22 HorseCroft Place, The
Pinnacles, Harlow, Essex,
CM19 5BX, 01279-626135

Mayhem Megastore
Pryors Farm, Patch Park,
Abridge Essex
014028-424; 014028-517

**Mayhem Pball
PowerGames**
The Power House Lewes
Rd. Blackboys Nr.
Uckfield
E. Sussex, TN22 5LG
01825-890-033

Mayhem Paintball
Midlands,172 Argyle St.
Cuckoo Bridge Ind'lEstate,
Nechells, Bham B7 5TE,
01435-866-189

Operation Paintball
Unit 23C,
Hagh Ln Ind East, Hexham
N Cumberland, NE46 3PU

Paintball Experience
27 Sidmouth St, Devizes
Wiltshire, SN10 1LD
01380-728-982

Paintball Planet
251 Deansgate
Manchester M34EN
44 (0) 161 839 2789

Paintball Planet
Unit 11 Millside Trdest.
Lawson Rd. Dartford Kent
DA1 5BH 44(0) 1322
222270

Paintball Sports
291 Deansgate
Manchester M3 4EW
0161-839-8493

Paintcheck Epsom
16 Beaconsfield Pl, Epsom
Surrey, KT17 4BD
01372-726-224

Pidley Paintball
49 Craitherne Way
North Arbury
Cambridgeshire, CB4 2LZ
01223-67665

Predator Paintball
14-16 Holbeach Rd.
Catford, London,
BR2 9NY
0181-690-7717

Pro-Line
8a Midas Bus. Cntr, Wantz
Rd, Dagenham, Essex,
RM10 8PS
0181-595-7771

QED Leisure
166 Lynne Road
Downham Market
Norfolk, PE38 9QG
01366-384-778

**Sheffield Paintball
Centre**
Unit C4, Main St
Hakenthorpe
Sheffield S12 4LB

Skirmish-Kent
The Holt, Church Ln,
Chelsham, Surrey, CR6
9PG 01883 627376

Skirmish-Nottingham
Unit 1, Wellbeck Ind Est,
Alfred Close,
Nottingham, NG3 1AD
01602 410 454

Survival Game
Canterbury, 52 Swale
Ave., Rushen-den,
Isle of Sheppey
Kent ME11 5JX,
01795-583-303

Survival Game/Frome
14 Arcacia Dr, Frome
Sommerset, BA11 2TS
01373-471-035

Survival Game (Staffs)
Painley Hill Farm
Bramshall, Uttoxeter
Staffordshire, ST14 8SQ
01889-502-508

Survival Game (SW)
Southdown Farm
Yarnscombe nr. Barnstable
N. Devon, EX31 3LZ
01271-858-279

**Survival Game West
Midlands**
c/o Daystate
Newcastle St., Stone
Staffordshire, ST15 8JU
01785-819-609

**Survival Game
(Yorks)Moore Farm**
Elsham near Brigg
S. Humberside
01652-688-912

Wigan Birds and Pets
80 Ormskirk Rd,
Newtown
Wigan, WN5 9EA, WDP

Unit 5, Metro Triangle
221 Mount St, Nechells
Birmingham, B7 5QT
0121-328-2228

SCOTLAND

Aberdeen Profields
Cullerlie By Skene
Aberdeenshire AB3 6XA
0133-08414

Alternative Leisure
East Woods Bus. Center
Green Hill Ave.
Glasgow, G46 6OX
01416 382-811

Edinburgh Profields
136A St. Johns Road
Edinburgh EH12 7SB
0131-316-4004

Maxamillion Events
Overton Cottage
Kirknewton
Midlothian, EH27 8DD
01506-884-088

Mayhem-Edinburgh
14 Ochiltree Ct, Mid
Calder Livingstone
W Lothian, Scotland EH53
ORU

SimulateD ActivitieS
4 Lochrin Place, Tollcross
Edinburgh, EH3 9QY
0131-2299827

WALES

Leisure Pursuits
Langrove Country Club,
Fairwood Common
Swansea, S. Wales
0144-128-2410

Paintball Consortium
53 Station Road, Deeside,
Clwyd, N Wales
01244-821490

SimulateD ActivitieS
19 Seymour St, Aberdare
Mid Glamorgan, CF44 7BL
01685-875-633

CANADA

ALBERTA

**Alan Kerr/Ty Cale
Security Equip.**
10769 99th St, Ed, Ata,
T5H 4H6, 403-424-8851

Edmonton Survival Game
4968 98th Ave,
Edmonton Alta, T6B 2Y7
403-469-4263

Pball Adventure World
1912 Mackay Rd. NW
Calgary, Alb, T3B 1C7
403-289-8887

Pursuit Supplies Int'l
5809 118th Ave, Ed.
Alberta, T5W 1E5
403-477-9252

Tactical Adventure Game
Box 344, Red Deer,
Alberta, T4N 5E9,
403-347-4444

Unique Outdoor Supplies
4968 98 Ave, Edmonton
Alberta, T6B 2Y7
403-469-4263

BRITISH COLUMBIA

Adrenaline Sports
1050 Saskatoon Ave.
Prince Rupert, BC V8J 4P1
604-627-7644

BC Elite Adventure Sports
16492 104th Ave
Surrey, BC, V4N 1Y5
604-951-0988

Frontline Paintball Supp
13377 72nd Ave.
Surray, BC CD V3W 2N5
604-501-0903

MANITOBA

Paintball Paradise
St. Laurent, Man. CD
204-338-1535
Nova Scotia

Banshee Paintball
122 Portland Street
Dartmouth, NS, B2Y 1H8
902-469-6926

L & M Surplus
1823 Sackville Drive
Mid. S'ville N S, B4C 257
902-865-6794

Spike's Action Games
416 Robie St. Truro, NS,
B2N 1L8, 902-893-8377,
897-7700

Wizard Paintball
11 Riverside Street
N Glasgow, NS, B2H 3S1
902-755-9904

ONTARIO

CD Paintball Supp
6 Brucedale Ave. West
Hamilton, Ont, L9C 1C2
416-383-9614

Flag-Grab Paintball
PO Box 30 RR#1
Lansdowne, Ont, K0E 1L0
613-659-4145

Premium Pball Products
371 Old Kingston Rd. #2
Scarborough Ont.
M1C 1B7
416-284-0746
888-236-6090

RLD Games Ltd.
350 Brawley Rd. West
Brooklin, Ont. CD
L0B 1C0
1-800-668-5809

Superior Paintball
94 Megginson Drive
Sault Ste. Marie, Ont.
P6A 6A9
705-946-8773

Triangle Computer & Hobby
6 George Street
Pt Colborne, Ont. L3K 3S1
905-834-4341

Ultimate Adventures
76 Cardish Street
Kleinburg, Ont L0J 1C0
905-893-1815

Wasaga Beach Pball
396 River Rd. West
Wasaga Bch, Ont. L0L 2P0
705-429-5065

QUEBEC

Adventure Division Ltd.
860 Bernard Pilon
McMasterville, QC
J3G 5W8
514-441-1129; 464-5639

Arnold Paintball
474 Chemin Covey Hill
Hemmingford, QC
514-949-8736

Le Jeu Survival I
Mansonville, QC
514-295-2706

Le Jeu Survival II
Iberville, QC
514-346-2709

PBL/PMI Canada East
8136 Jean Brillon
La Salle, QC H8N 2J5
514-595-5993

Quebec Paintball
800 Chemin de la
Canardiere, QC G1J 2B7
418-623-4496

SASKATCHEWAN

Adventure Co. Paintball
2713 45th A Ave
Lloydminster, Sk., S9V 1A6
306-825-7902

Moosehorn Pball Games
Box 278
Maidstone, Sk, S0M 1M0
306-893-2912

Pball Action Games
Box 454
Asquith, Sask, S0K 0J0
306-329-4290

AUSTRALIA

NEW SOUTH WALES

Adventure Quest Games
19 Sommerset Street
Epping, Sydney 2121
02-876-6382

Aussie Paintball Game
201 Canterbury
Bankstown, NSW 2200
02-790-1401

Hamsta Where? Action Apparel
18 Brunker Rd.
Greenacre NSW 2190
02 796 8536

Impact Paintball
102 The Esplanade
Ettalong Beach 2257
02-43-413-829

Phantom Zone
93A Argyle St.
Parramatta 2150
02-891-1848

Skirmish Adventures
Head Office
Level 2, 18 Brunker Rd.
Greenacre NSW 2190
02 796 7955, 02 796 8397

Finding Paintball

Skirmish Adventures
Pinch Hill Hume Hwy.
Gunning, NSW 2581
1 800 63 62 61

Skirmish Adventures
Lawrence Hargreave Dr.
Helensburgh, Sydney
N.S.W. 2190 Australia
1 800 63 62 61

QUEENSLAND

Pball Australia Pty. Ltd.
Gold Coast War Museum
Springbrook Rd., Mud-
geeraba Gold Coast 4213
07-5-305222

Samford Skirmish
Samford Rd. Samford
4520
07-289-1820

Skirmish Adventures
Bowhunters Rd.
Townesville, Qld. 4810
02 796 2671

Skirmish Sunshine Coast
Ettamogah Pub Aussie
Village, Bruce Hwy,
Palmview, Sunshine Coast
07-4-94-5566

Top Gun Paintball Fields
Glengarry Rd.
Keperra 4054
07-392-0022

Top Gun Paintball Fields
Cedar Creek Lodge
Thunderbird Park, Mt.
Tamborine Qld.
07-392-0022

SOUTH AUSTRALIA

Skirmish
Mary St., Unley 5061
08-371-0776

VICTORIA

Pball Skirmish Games
1175 High Street
Armdale, Victoria 3143
03 822 1100

Skirmish Survival Games
35 Spring St.
Sandringham 3191
018-370-390

WORLDWIDE

BRAZIL

**Mercenarios Pball
Supply**
Shopping Center Lapa
Rua Catao, 72-Lj. K-18
05049-901 S. Paulooo-SP
Brazil
01155-11 3871 1468

Wargames Paintball
Target Emp. Com. Field &
Supply, Av. Brig. Luis
Antonio 478 5° and
Sao Paulo, 01426
01155-11 232-5470

CURACAO

Bad Boyz Toyz Curacao
Caracasbaaiweg #164
Esther Blds. Unit 8
Curacao, Netherlands
Antilles 5999-4656402,
5999-4658550 fax

Bad Boyz Toyz Curacao
Sup'Air Ball Field,
Rust&Burgh Asiento
Sport Complex, Curacao,
Netherlands Antilles
5999-4656402, 5999-
4658550

CZECH REPUBLIC

Survival Games Bohemia
Jana Masaryka 26 Praha 2
Czech Republic 120 00
042 2 691 0843

DENMARK

Action Pursuit Centre
Nybrovej 304 C5, DK-
2800, Lyngby
8781211 31535511

Arms Gallary City
Nybrogade 26
1203 Kobenhavn K
33-118-338

Danish Paintball
østerbro 37A
9000 Aalborg, 98 124277

Danish Paintball
Frederiksgade 72 Kld
8000 Aarhus C, 86 98937

Shoot to Thrill
Amagerbrogade 220 B
DK-2300 Copenhagen S
45 32 97 44 04

Proline Scandinavia A/S
Yderlandsvej 25
Kobenhavn S 2300
45 3154 2045

FRANCE

CAMP
64 rue des mathurins
75008 Paris France
01.42.68.10.00;
01.42.68.12.96 fx

F.L.A.G.
1 rue du Rocher
78610 St-Leger-En-Yvelines
34.86.33.14

Skirmish France
Domaine de Bousserain
71320 Toulon
Sur Arroux,France
01033 85795148

GERMANY

Brass Eagle Germany
Rainer Ehrig-Braun
Siegfried-Leopoldstr. 5
5300 Bonn-Beuel
0228-473205

Doc's Paintball Shop
Myhler Straße 19
27711 Osterholz-
Scharmbeck
04791/89 136,

**Farbdschungel Furth
P'ball Gear**
Elsternstr. 3a
Tuch-enbach 90587
0911 7568 212

HarBur Marketing Inc.
Auf der Pick 5
D-66849 Landstuhl 49
Germany 06371 60291;
06371 912310 fx

JM SchieB-Sport-Bedarf
Postfach 5843, D-8700
Wurzburg 09302-846

**Kaiserslautern Rod &
Gun Club**
86 SVS SVBH, Unit 3240,
Box 535, APO, AE 09094
49-631-57484

Kotte & Zeller
Industristr. 415 65,
W-95365 Rugendorf
092-21-84034

OPM Paintball Supplies
Ronsdorferstr. 143,
Tor 11 40233 Dusseldorf
0211-733-3155

Paintball Consortium
Holderlinsallee 6
2000 Hamburg 60
40-279-45-65

Paintball Special Sports
PO Box 6532, D 4400
Munster, 0251-55503

Paintball Sports Germany
Kleine Pfaffengasse 3
67346 Speyer
06232 / 620571

Venom, The Toxic Toys
Lohbecker Berg 18
45470 Muhlheim an
der Ruhr
0208-380280

GREECE

Voyager Adventure Games
25 Sigala Street
542 48 Thessaloniki
30 31 325833

HOLLAND

ASCO Sports-Inc.
Hoefblad 12
1911 PA Uitgeest
0-2513-20420

ASCO Sports Paintball Games
Ned., Hoefblad 12
1911 PA Uitgeest
0-2513-14870

ASCO Paintball Games
1e Middellandstraat 104b
3021 BH Rotterdam,
010-4778979

Euro Pball Adventures
Marimbastraat 6
5802 LW Venray
04780-87087

Jobs Paintball Shop
William De Zwijgerlaan
71-73
1056-JG, Amsterdam
020-850-700

The Old Man Hardware
Damstraat 16
Amsterdam 1012 2M
020 627 0043

Realistic Fantasies Pball
Erasmusgracht 5, 1056BB
Amsterdam, Holland
020-683-6474

Splat Attack
Schenkkade 293-294
2595 AX's-Gravenhage
31-0-70-385-6699

Stichting Paintball Limburg
Dwarsstraat 27, 6361 XM
Nuth.
31-45-244385

IRELAND

Escarmouche Paintball
Belfast 327500, SimulateD
ActivitieS
Cork, Ireland
150-4624

Skirmish Ireland Cranwell
Rockville Crescent
Blackrock, Dublin Eire
010353 12819009

ISRAEL

Israel Paintball Games
PO Box 53052
Tel Aviv, Israel 61530
972-3-482653

ITALY

Associazione Giochi Sopravvivenza
PO Box 38
21020 Casciqago-Va

Survival Game Sport Adventures,
F.I.G.P., Via Strada del
Trombone, 14, 44013
Consandolo FE
39-532 858145, 337 590589

JAPAN

International Paint-ball Game Federation Japan
1024 Kamikasuya Isehara,
Kanagawa 259-11
81-463-87-5895

J.P.P.L.
7-1 Yama Iwadecho
Nagagun
Wakayama 649-62
81-736-61-6322

KOREA

Asia Pacific Int'l
Keoyang Bldg. Rm. 202
#51-8, Susongdong,
Chongno Gu, Seoul,
Korea 110-140
82-2-734-9130

MEXICO

Chango's Army
Aeropuerto Atizapan
Distrito Federal, Mexico
525-519-0303

NEW ZEALAND

Super Splat (NZ) Ltd.
241 Blenheim Rd.
PO Box 22662,
Christchurch
64 03 343-3055

NORWAY

IB Paintball,
Vogts Gate 39, 0444
Oslo 4
47-22-718102

Paintball Centre
Ostifaret 10
1476 Rasta, Norway
47-2-700-130

PANAMA

Sports International
Via Brasil, Building #38,
Local #24, 6-9425 El
Dorado, Panama 265-0625

PHILIPPINES

Gotcha, Inc.
291 P. Guevarra Ave
San Juan Metro Manilla
011-63-2-70-64-47

ROMANIA

Mercenars Club
B-dul 1 mai nr. 29
B.PF9 ScB. Ap.35
Constanta cod 8700
004041587592;
fax 004041545226;
GSM 092752454

RUSSIA

Action Paintball Games
20-2 Panfilova str,
Moscow, 125080, Russia
095-785-1762
095-796-4646

Paintland Paintball Sports Club
Kalashny pereulok, 10,
Moscow, 095-918-4580,
291-2259

Russian National P'ball Association
5 Kozuhovskaia
Moscow 22-1-60
095-277-7424, 166-6200

SLOVENIA

Soberl d.o.o.
Rosinova 3
Maribor, Slovenia 62 000
62 413 946

SOUTH AFRICA

IMEXO
PO Box 7216, Roggebaal
Cape Town 8001, SA
021-701-5941

Indoor Paintball City
7 Du Preez Street, Knights
1413 Johanesburg, So.
Africa
011-828-7583

Paintball Supplies
PO Box 3090, Symridge
1420 Johanesburg, So.
Africa
011-828-7583

SWEDEN

Paintball Sports
Bispmotalagaten 7
591 30 Motala
0141-55550

Tradition Sturegallerian
114 46 Stockholm
08-611-45-35

Tradition Femmanhuset
411 06 Goteborg
031-15-03-66

THAILAND

International Paintball Club
437-118 Soi Yodsak
Pattaya, Thailand
(66) 01-919-2635

VENEZUELA

Estrategia
C.C. Multicentro 1er Piso
Local 26 Cagua, Aragua,
2122
044-960455, 044
99577970

Paintball Sport de
Venezuela Ave.
Francisco di Miranda,
Centro Plaza, Niveo
Jardin, Local CC-322-A,
Los Palos Grandes,
Caracus, Venezuela
582-286-4483

Survival Games Club, CA
Calle Baruta con
Los Cerritos
Res. Paso Real #18
Caracas,